the leadership game

DR DAMIEN BARRY

the leadership game

**STRATEGIES FOR SUCCESS IN
THE SCHOOL LEADERSHIP ARENA**

This book is dedicated to my first principal, Mrs Deborah Kachel.

From 1997 to 1999, I spent my first years as a young teacher of science, geography, and health and physical education at Mossman State High School on the edge of the Daintree Rainforest.

Deborah, you were the epitome of kindness, grace, humility, wisdom and strength.

I didn't know it at the time, but I was so lucky to have you as my principal, mentor and friend.

Thank you!

Published in 2024 by Amba Press, Melbourne, Australia
www.ambapress.com.au

© Damien Barry 2024

All rights reserved. No part of this book may be reproduced or transmitted in any form or by any means, electronic or mechanical, including photocopying, recording or by any information storage and retrieval system, without prior permission in writing from the publisher.

Cover design: Tess McCabe
Internal design: Amba Press
Editor: Francesca Hoban Ryan

ISBN: 9781923116474 (pbk)
ISBN: 9781923116481 (ebk)

A catalogue record for this book is available from the National Library of Australia.

Contents

Preface		1
Introduction		7
1	On leadership	11
2	The new guy or gal	23
3	Seats on the bus	27
4	The power of community	31
5	The purpose of a vision	37
6	The importance of visibility	45
7	Difficult conversations	49
8	Building your team	55
9	Self-care: Slay the beast and avoid burnout	61
10	Resource management: Things that open and shut	69
11	Leading staff	79
12	Leading students	87
13	Leading parents	95
14	The Wisdom story: A case study	103
15	The future of school leadership	125
Conclusion		135
The 15 rules of the leadership game		139
References		141
Acknowledgements		143
About the author		145

Preface

My plan wasn't to become a teacher. In fact, I had my heart set on being a policeman. Assuming I'd get shot as soon as I started, Mum and Dad were less than encouraging; apparently I'd done enough during my teenage years to justify their lack of faith. It became evident that the police force was not my destiny when I was politely told—as a 17-year-old applicant who didn't have a driver's licence, couldn't hold a firearm without shaking, barely passed the physical exam and was even discouraged from joining by his local sergeant to come back in a few years. Luckily, my acceptance into a secondary teaching undergraduate degree came through at roughly the same time. With Mum and Dad packing my suitcase as a not-too-subtle hint to get my backside on the road and no other clear options in front of me, a teaching career it was.

After finishing my degree in 1996, I commenced my career in 1997 at Mossman State High School, a medium-sized public secondary school about an hour's drive north of Cairns in Far North Queensland, just on the edge of the Daintree Rainforest. With its semi-rural position, small-town locality and community vibe, it had a great bunch of teachers across the career spectrum. Mossman provided me with strong role models, mentors and an excellent foundation to my career. I saw what good teaching looked like and how good teachers prepared, planned, interacted, assessed, provided feedback and generally organised themselves. Mossman also provided an environment for me to try things beyond the classroom: organising camps, writing up work programs, leading large-scale sporting carnivals, and being part of professional and community groups. I absolutely loved it.

After the crucible of my first year, I was lucky enough to be given opportunities for small leadership positions that included year-level and subject co-ordinator roles. I spent three years at Mossman before moving to Brisbane to continue my career, eventually taking on leadership roles including head of department, head of middle school, head of senior school and deputy headmaster.

Over the past 10 years I've been a principal across two schools. I've experienced highs and lows. I've been able to work with amazing people, open new campuses, travel the world, lead exciting initiatives and implement change with a profound impact on students and colleagues. I've also had personal relationship breakdowns, an addiction to alcohol and the experience of weight gain, depression, anxiety and self-doubt. Maybe it was inevitable that these afflictions would emerge after bubbling under the surface, but the pressure of principalship certainly enabled and accelerated the process.

I could see a cycle of negativity play out on a weekly basis, but I was incapable of stopping it. It often started with insecurity about my ability (imposter syndrome) or negative self-talk around a difficult conversation. This fed my anxiety and depression, causing me to withdraw from my personal relationships. In turn, my withdrawal led to excessive drinking and then to more weight gain and depression.

While stuck in this negative cycle, I was trying to run a school, be a rock for other staff and a smiling face at assembly, raise my own family and continue to study. That was how I thought I could mitigate my self-doubt and insecurity. I lost count of how many times I thought of leaving the profession, or at least taking a step away from a leadership role and going back full-time to my 'happy place' in the classroom.

Anyway, I stayed in the role and the profession. Maybe it was maturity, more time in the seat or my own kids growing up. Maybe it was feeling more comfortable in my own skin as I approached the big 5-0. One day I decided to not wrap myself up in my job so much, and to start prioritising my health—physical and emotional. I set myself a few goals and challenges. I decided to stop being so hard on myself. I stopped drinking. I lost weight. I made time for the gym. I started trail running. I started to pursue other hobbies like creative writing. I reconnected with old friends. I nurtured my close personal relationships. I connected with nature. I do regress at times, but I get back on track quickly. I remind myself that consistency, not perfection, is my goal.

My desire now is to help other educators become better teachers and school leaders. Modern-day schools are like organisations with hundreds if not thousands of employees, all crammed onto the same patch of soil for extended periods of time. Not all of these people are rational, mature, balanced adults: they range in age from about 5 to 65. Some—the teenagers—are in the most tumultuous times of their lives. These organisations operate in an occasionally high-risk environment that requires their employees to move around throughout the day and change tasks on the hour. They demand compliance from many whose reluctance to be there is revealed through indifference or outright hostility. Fundamental to its existence are staff of differing opinions and competencies, but also parents who remain largely external. All of this occurs against a backdrop of social, political and economic pressures. School leadership is awash with challenges, and those charged with bringing some order to this rabble need to make it as safe and worthwhile as possible.

Each of my many and varied leadership experiences has taught me something new. Perhaps the most challenging responsibility to date has been my current job of leading a single-campus school located in a complex multicultural context, with students drawn from over 40 cultural and ethnic backgrounds. I have also led a school with multiple campuses spread across two states. I have been a deputy headmaster at an all-boys school, a head of middle school at a large co-ed independent school, and a head of department and head of sport at an all-girls school. I have taught and held leadership roles across a diverse range of schools: public, Anglican, Presbyterian and Methodist, Uniting Church, Exclusive (Plymouth) Brethren and Islamic-inspired. My experience has well and truly run the gamut, and I have acquired some hard-earned wisdom along the way. Would I do it all again? You bet. I hope, however, that it wouldn't take me until almost 50 years of age to learn how to look after myself. It is in this spirit that I now wish to share with other school leaders—current and aspiring—some practical words of guidance that will steer them on the path to success.

The 17 lessons of the leadership game

1. To enter the leadership arena means that you don't merely endure the battle. It means that you embrace it and everything that comes with it—the good and the bad, especially the bad.
2. There are different leadership styles, and different contexts require different leaders. Find your own style but recognise what your context requires from you and adapt accordingly.
3. Whether you've been externally or internally appointed to your new leadership role, it's important to start off by revealing not only your vision and intent but also who you are as a person. Don't dampen your audience's enthusiasm with detail and dullness; lift their spirits with aspiration and ambition.
4. Your school is a bus, and you're driving it. Your first job is to get the seats sorted. Move the right people into those seats. Escort off the bus those who cannot or will not buckle up. Provide good service to the people who buy a ticket to ride.
5. A school is strong when the community that surrounds it is strong. Look for ways to build connections, relationships and partnerships. Be deliberate and persistent in this task.
6. A vision is the ultimate aspirational goal for your school, the foundation upon which everything else is built. Alignment with the classroom is critical: you don't want your vision to be a bunch of nebulous flowery words that nobody buys into.

7. Get comfortable with being visible. Visibility does more than put a face to a name—it builds your understanding of the organisation and everyone else's trust in you.
8. No-one likes to have difficult conversations, but avoiding them means endorsing bad behaviour, killing morale, lowering standards and losing good people.
9. Build your team with mutual respect and clear expectations, and allow them to do the same with their teams. It's one of the most powerful ways to achieve your collective organisational goals.
10. Self-care is a regular meeting with yourself that might just save not only your health, but also your career, your family and your life.
11. As dull as it might sound, resource management is a critical part of school leadership. People don't notice when it's working, but they sure as hell do when it isn't. When not done well, it can bring a school to its knees.
12. The quickest way to lose the trust of your staff is to ask them to do something that you either can't or won't do yourself. Do the hard carry.
13. If you and your staff aren't united in your approach to leading students, you're wasting your time. Don't be that person who tries to be liked by the kids only to undermine your colleagues.
14. Facilities are nice, but they are less important than the level of genuine care that teachers and leaders have for a child.
15. When building or rebuilding a school, start with people first and structures second. Systems, platforms and frameworks should come last. If you don't know what you want the school to stand for, you can't put things in place to help you get there.
16. The future of schooling will see institutional shackles broken to create greater flexibility, choice and partnerships. Just as the classroom silo has opened up, so too in time will the school silo.
17. Good leadership is an accumulation of interactions and decisions that build people, strengthen relationships, and provide stability and direction.

Introduction

***Lesson #1** To enter the leadership arena means that you don't merely endure the battle. It means that you embrace it and everything that comes with it—the good and the bad, especially the bad.*

The Leadership Game is more than a book about leadership. It's an instruction manual on how to do leadership. It is my belief that the skills, techniques and nuances of leadership can be taught and applied. Leaders are shaped over time through exposure and experience, wins and defeats. As I revealed about teaching in my first book, *The Teaching Game*, leadership is governed by certain rules that, once known, can be played like a game. I don't mean a game in the sense of a frivolous thing to be played for fun—quite the contrary. The game of leadership is vitally important for the livelihoods, careers, wellbeing and futures of many people who rely on leaders to get things right.

We've all seen what happens when leadership fails. Sometimes it takes years for an organisation to regain balance, harmony and success. Good people leave, toxic cultures dominate, inefficiencies and failures become the norm, sharing and collaboration dry up, high levels of sickness emerge, innovation is hobbled and there's no celebration, acknowledgment or joy. Successful leadership takes courage, conviction, humility and the ability to bounce back. Decisions are executed in the best interests of everyone, even when they are terribly difficult to make. People celebrate the success of others, and they share and collaborate constantly. Mistakes are treated as learning opportunities. Leaders really listen, engage, include and discuss. Mentoring is prolific, innovation encouraged and supported.

We all know the traits and characteristics of successful leaders; every second LinkedIn post seems to list them. Why, then, do so many people and organisations get it wrong? The act of leading is not as simple as reading something and thinking: 'Yep, I can do this integrity thing' or 'I'm inclusive and collaborative' or 'I'm empathetic and humble'. Leadership is a series of specific little things done day after day over a long period of time in the face of setbacks, uncertainty, failure, undermining, self-doubt and sometimes outright sabotage. Aspiring leaders have to be ready to learn. They have to be thick-skinned and tenacious, prepared to play hard in the arena.

You may have noticed that I've mentioned the concept of the leadership arena a few times now. 'Arena' conjures up an image of a gladiatorial venue or sporting stadium, a place where combatants come together to battle it out. A winner and a loser will emerge after significant warfare, bloodshed or competition involving pain and anguish. In the adversarial context of a school, it is not a physical battle that ensures but one of viewpoints and beliefs, opinions, ego, competency and sometimes self-interest.

In 1910, one year after leaving his office as President of the United States, Theodore Roosevelt delivered a speech known as *Citizenship in a Republic* to an audience at the Sorbonne in Paris. There is one notable passage that endures to this day, and it is called 'The Man in the Arena':

> *It is not the critic who counts; not the man who points out how the strong man stumbles, or where the doer of deeds could have done them better. The credit belongs to the man who is actually in the arena, whose face is marred by dust and sweat and blood; who strives valiantly; who errs, who comes short again and again, because there is no effort without error and shortcoming; but who does actually strive to do the deeds; who knows great enthusiasms, the great devotions; who spends himself in a worthy cause; who at the best knows in the end the triumph of high achievement, and who at the worst, if he fails, at least fails while daring greatly, so that his place shall never be with those cold and timid souls who neither know victory nor defeat.*

School leadership is certainly at times a very difficult vocation, and arguably is becoming even more so. A leader may find themselves in the midst of it all trying to forge ahead, making mistakes along the way yet pushing on because they feel called to realise their passion for educating students and guiding people towards success.

This book is written to provide an insight into the life of a principal and what it takes to lead and manage a school. It can just as equally be applied to other significant educational leadership roles. The chapters are grouped around core aspects of school leadership with commentary on staff, students, parents and community. They also include reflections and strategies for topics that are equally important but for some reason not usually canvassed: what to do if you are new to a leadership role, the importance of organisational structures, how to manage resources and practice self-care. One chapter is devoted to a case study of my current school at the time of writing: Wisdom College, a P–12 school on the south side of Brisbane. Wisdom is a wonderfully vibrant multicultural community in which I feel very fortunate to play a role. I believe that if I am to offer advice and suggestions on school leadership, then I should have lived and breathed the successes and challenges myself. I hope you find my experience useful.

1

On leadership

Lesson #2 *There are different leadership styles, and different contexts require different leaders. Find your own style but recognise what your context requires from you and adapt accordingly.*

Maybe you are a classroom teacher with a few years of experience, and you have a desire for something more in your career. At this stage, your aspiration might not necessarily be for principalship. It may simply be to lead a project, a small subject team, a year level, a department, a pastoral care group. If this is you, ask yourself two questions first.

Am I a competent teacher?

Can you confidently give useful feedback, and will others listen to you because they trust your ability and advice? If you can't do at least a decent job of carrying out the core function of the schooling system, then you certainly are not ready for more.

What is my motivation for leadership?

This is a hard-look-in-the-mirror question. If the answer has more to do with feeding your ego, then you are seeking leadership for all the wrong reasons and will not be successful. If the answer involves enabling others, effecting positive change, creating innovative learning environments or making a difference in the lives of students, then you're on the right track. This tells me that as a leader, you will place your needs second to those of the people you serve. If you're interested in learning more, I suggest reading *Leaders Eat Last* by business leadership expert Simon Sinek.

Hopefully your aspiration for leadership is a noble one. What next? Broadly speaking, you will develop your skills through the following avenues of leadership opportunity or on-the-job training.

The first avenue is to lead a project, an activity or an event. If anyone else is directly involved, they will have a clearly defined role without as much impact. For instance, you might take responsibility for the writing of Year 7 maths assessments or for the Year 9 pastoral care program. You might organise the logistics of the outdoor education program and sort out venues, transport, permission forms and risk assessments.

The second avenue involves people. For example, creating a school-wide literacy framework or developing a behaviour-management policy—these activities require you to get others to buy in, to do significant jobs for the benefit of others, to act as a team. You don't need to be a Rhodes Scholar to recognise that Avenue 2 is the trickier of the pair. Whenever people are involved, a job becomes harder. Large projects often involve a number of people from different segments of a school. Some of these people may not want to be part of your team, and others will already have a distaste for the project. This is when your leadership skills will be most needed and quickly developed.

One thing no-one tells you about school leadership is that if you have your own classes, they will come last. You will be constantly busy organising everyone and everything else. This is another reason why you'd better be a very good teacher with plenty of skill, experience and resources at your fingertips.

My suggestion is to start small and simple. If you are fortunate enough to be able to pick and choose opportunities, then select one with minimal moving parts. With this approach you can at least learn some skills alongside your existing workload. It will teach you time management, prioritisation and core project management without the hassle of excessive meetings and group communication, or the need to rely on others or massage egos. Once you've had some experience with this type of leadership or project management and find that you enjoy it, then seek out something that involves other people. Hopefully you have a senior leadership team who can provide you with mentoring along the way.

If you are truly genuine about leadership, then initially you will need to take on opportunities without the expectation of remuneration or time off in lieu. The rewards will come in due course, as long as you do a good job. You also need to realise that no-one is going to seek you out to hand you a leadership gig; you have to ask to take things on. Most colleagues will wet themselves with gratitude if you offer to help without expectation of reward.

You are responsible for your own career. You might be lucky enough to have a thoughtful mentor who knows you well, is aware of your aspirations, vouches for you and pushes you towards roles. If not, go get it yourself! Only you really know what you want.

This brings me to my final point: perhaps you have a yearning for leadership but are unsure which path to take. Curriculum? Pastoral? Administrative? Co-curricular? Just choose one. If you don't like it, use your newfound experience to pursue the path meant for you. As Andy Dufresne and Ellis 'Red' Redding say in the movie *The Shawshank Redemption*, 'get busy living or get busy dying'.

Becoming a leader

When I look back on my first day in the seat as a school principal, I realise I did not fully appreciate the level of responsibility that came with the role. I also didn't grasp the various hats that a principal has to wear on a daily basis. I understood the magnitude of my obligations to staff and students in previous leadership roles, but deep down I always knew that someone else had ultimate accountability and liability. My principals had afforded me a cushion of managerial oversight.

The initiatives I was charged with implementing usually did not arise at my own suggestion. Some were part of a strategic or operational plan mandated by a systemic head office or department, and some were decided upon by the school board, the principal or the senior leadership team. Most of the time, I believed in the merits of the project and did my duty with the requisite gusto.

When I became a principal, it was suddenly all on me. Sure, I had a supportive board and an excellent team of colleagues, but I was very aware of my responsibility to everyone around me. If you read the job description of a principal, you will find it doesn't quite tell the true story. Phrases like 'communicate effectively with key stakeholders', 'provide pedagogical leadership', 'manage the human resources of the organisation' and 'oversee the capital works program' cannot realistically convey the complexity of the tasks they describe. What do they really mean?

The job description

This is my plain-language job description for the modern-day principal. Like many school leaders, I teach a class—let's assume that the role here doesn't include a teaching component.

Teaching and learning

The principal will:

- Provide overall responsibility for student care, discipline and learning
- Ensure that educational programs (including curricular and co-curricular) are developed, implemented and reviewed
- Ensure that wellbeing programs are written, implemented and reviewed to provide high-level social and emotional instruction to all students

What does this mean? It means you must ensure that the staff charged with writing and delivering the curriculum are getting it done. This includes the Australian Curriculum from Prep to Year 10, the requisite state-based curriculum in Years 11 and 12, pastoral care programs and vocational courses and training. It also means that a behaviour-management strategy must be in place and enacted.

Administration and operations

The principal will:

- Provide oversight of all school accreditation requirements (for public, Catholic and independent sectors)
- Ensure that the school has marketing, promotions and enrolment plans and that these are implemented
- Implement a staff culture of workplace health and safety (WHS) and risk management, ensuring that risks are identified, mitigated and reviewed
- Implement a robust policy and procedure for child safety and protection
- Ensure that the daily operations of the school are such that the school is fully operational, that daily relief is managed, that timetables are functional, that the LMS (Learning Management System) and SMS (School Management System) are functional

What does this mean? It means that the principal must ensure on a daily basis that the school is safe and ready to go with the fundamental elements that allow it to operate effectively. It means that core platforms, processes, systems and procedures must be in place, functional and supporting all staff in their roles. It doesn't mean that the principal does all the heavy lifting with timetables and policies, but it does mean that those responsible are getting it done.

Facilities

The principal will:

- Ensure that the school has the classrooms required to deliver the curriculum, including science labs, art rooms, hospitality facilities and technology labs
- Ensure that the school has the appropriate fields, courts and facilities to conduct sporting and artistic lessons, competitions and activities
- Provide sufficient shade, seating and storage for all students, staff and visitors
- Ensure that WHS is catered for across all facilities to provide a safe environment for students, staff, parents and visitors

- Implement a process to future-proof the school in terms of projected repairs, maintenance and replacement needs
- Fulfil the IT needs for all sectors of the school to support teaching and learning

What does this mean? It means that the principal must make sure that the school has enough classroom, sporting and learning spaces and equipment for all students and staff, and that these are safe and comfortable. It means that there are enough laptops for everyone, that the internet is stable, and that things like firewalls are in place.

Parents and community

The principal will:

- Cultivate a strong Parents and Friends (P&F) Committee that provides support to the school and is a communication avenue for parents and guardians
- Ensure multiple communication channels for parents to stay informed, seek feedback, contact staff and stay abreast of the progress of their children
- Build a community of trust and partnership with parents and the wider community to ensure that feedback is heard and enacted, that school initiatives are strengthened and that learning is positively impacted

What does this mean? It means that the principal must forge strong partnerships with parents and continuously look at ways to keep them informed, with the aim of using their help in all sorts of events and co-curricular activities. It means that a variety of communication mechanisms are deployed and that information is timely and correct.

Governance

The principal will:

- Provide monthly reports to the board
- Keep the board chair informed of significant items related to strategy, staffing and risk

- Write annual reports and fiduciary and compliance reports for external bodies
- Implement board policies and strategic decisions
- Ensure policy development, renewal and implementation

What does this mean? It means that the principal will manage up and down to be the instrument of the board when it comes to strategy and board decisions, and will ensure that the school is compliant and up-to-date with all necessary policies.

Budgets and finances

The principal will:

- Set tuition fees, including levies, in partnership with the board
- Set salaries, including the provision of appropriate superannuation and leave entitlements for all staff, in partnership with the board
- Ensure that the school remains solvent, is able to pay its bills on time, can manage its cash flow, and prepares and administers an annual budget

What does this mean? The business or finance manager should be able to manage most of this, but the principal should ensure that it gets done in a prudent and responsible manner with board input, and that staff and parents are suitably informed. There is no point in having grand plans for facilities if salaries can't be paid. The principal must set priorities for spending and be comfortable in saying no.

Staff

The principal will:

- Oversee the selection, appointment, induction, management and termination of all staff
- Provide a framework for the wellbeing of staff
- Oversee the appraisal process and professional learning program
- Ensure adequate staff for the needs of the school (e.g. a workforce plan)

What does this mean? Not all schools have a human resources department, and many of these duties will fall to the principal and/or deputy. It means that all aspects of staffing need to be managed, and that the wellbeing of staff is just as important as their ability to teach effectively.

Culture and climate

Finally, the big one that is almost impossible to capture in a job description: the role of the principal in establishing the culture and climate of a school. This is difficult to articulate, and even harder to implement. Operational tasks can be written and pushed out, but the ability to create an environment that has high trust, collegiality and harmony? That's the stuff that really matters.

Leadership vs management

I've found over the years that I do as much management as I do leadership. There is a distinction: depending on its size, maturity and number of executive staff, a school will require different things from a principal. A large, well-established school will require its principal to focus on governance, setting a vision and leading the entire school community towards the fulfilment of this vision; most of the operational stuff will be done by others. A start-up school or a small school will need a more hands-on principal. In this situation you may find yourself devising everything from timetables to playground duty rosters and strategic plans, in tandem with board members who lack experience in school governance. As you can perhaps tell, I am experienced in the latter!

You will no doubt have seen a schematic like the diagram below showing the distinction between leadership and management. There are dozens of these, and leadership books are littered with them.

LEADERSHIP	MANAGEMENT
Focuses on people	Focuses on things & tasks
Creates a vision	Executes a plan
Looks to the future	Looks at the present
Empowers & builds	Controls & measures
Influences & inspires	Demands & checks

This is rather simplistic, as most people in leadership do plenty of management tasks. To show the distinction between leadership and management for a principal, I have created the diagram below. Not every school is the same, so this diagram is quite generalist in nature.

LEADERSHIP (PEOPLE & STRATEGY FOCUS)
Coaches & develops people
Models desired behaviour
Drives change
Creates a vision
Develops strategy
Builds the school brand and reputation
Cultivates relationships, networks & partnerships
Promotes & represents the school in the community
Promotes the faith / values of the school
Cultivates culture, collaboration & collegiality

MANAGEMENT (PROCESS & TASK FOCUS)
Bridging the gap between board & staff
Establishing the master plan
Timetabling & staffing
Child safety, accreditation, compliance, workplace health & safety
Budgets, marketing & enrolments
Policies & procedures
Operational plan & daily operations
Curriculum & extra-curricular

Leadership styles

You may have heard of the more common leadership styles: servant leader, instructional leader, transactional leader, transformational leader. There are plenty more labels, many of which mean the same thing. Some management guru somewhere is always deciding to create a new label or tweak an existing one! The table below provides a very brief summary of the six most commonly recognised leadership styles, with a particular focus on what we might expect to see at a school.

Style	Summary	Characteristics	Pros	Cons	When best applied
Autocratic	Demands compliance	Stern, demanding	Makes decisions quickly	Discourages group input. Does not build a team.	Critical situations. When decisions can't be made. When leadership has been too casual or laissez-faire.
Democratic	Participative form of leadership	Collaborative, considerate, inclusive	Improves engagement	Can be slow to make decisions	When staff need to feel included and heard. When you need to get people on board.
Transformational (aka visionary)	Inspiring, high-motivation leadership	Extroverted, high-energy, charismatic	Can unite people. Can bring people with them on the journey.	Staff may already be change-fatigued	Great for change management and for growth periods

Style	Summary	Characteristics	Pros	Cons	When best applied
Transactional (similar to democratic)	Leader offers something in return	Uses a system of reward and consequence	Fair and relational	Overly bureaucratic and administrative	Great for when structures and frameworks need to be implemented
Servant (aka affiliative)	Believes in people first. Prioritises the greater good.	Trusting, unselfish mindset, builds others up	Builds trust. Employees feel valued. Shared vision.	Some staff are given too much responsibility. Slow to make decisions.	When staff need to feel valued. When you are trying to create a shared vision.
Instructional (aka coaching)	When a more experienced person provides support, guidance, mentoring or coaching	Nurturing, affirming, mentoring	A focus on the student and their learning. A desire to improve teacher competence.	More focused on the classroom than on the whole school. Can be overly prescriptive.	When there is a need for a clear focus on the quality of teaching and learning

A principal will need to adopt different leadership styles to suit their audience, their team and the task at hand. This is another unique aspect of principalship: the audience is never the same. I suppose other industries have their own audience segments to which the CEO or GM would need to tailor their communication, but a principal can rarely move across a single school day without having to occupy various leadership personas.

A typical day for me is very operational and transactional, relational and responsive. The transformational stuff will occur throughout the day when I am talking about a vision or strategy at the staff meeting, modelling expectations in the playground, coaching a colleague or speaking at assembly. Transformational leadership will also reveal itself in the way that I try to build trust and collegiality with the ground staff and admin staff. Instructional leadership will occur when I teach a class, visit classrooms or mentor a young teacher. Servant leadership happens when I am in the playground picking up litter with staff and students or responding to emails before bed so that others have the decisions they need by the time they start in the morning.

Key takeaway

Seeking to become a leader should not be an easy decision. Prepare to keep up your knowledge, your energy and your good humour. If it's a principalship that you seek, you'll need to accept that the buck stops with you. Start small by building relationships, expertise and a track record in an area you're comfortable in. You'll soon find out whether you're in it for the right reasons.

2

The new guy or gal

Lesson #3 *Whether you've been externally or internally appointed to your new leadership role, it's important to start off by revealing not only your vision and intent but also who you are as a person. Don't dampen your audience's enthusiasm with detail and dullness; lift their spirits with aspiration and ambition.*

There are two ways to be elevated into a senior leadership role at a school: as an external appointment or as an internal appointment. The reaction of a school community to a newly-appointed leader will be affected by their relationship with the person previously in the role (and of course with the new leader if they were already employed at the school). If the predecessor was much loved and admired, their replacement will at first face inevitable comparisons. If they were unpopular, it might make things easier. Whatever the case, each new leader must forge their own identity.

Whether you aspire to establish yourself in a leadership position at a new school or at your current school, here are some words of advice.

External appointment

The external appointment is always given a grace period, also known as a honeymoon period. In the political world this is generally known to be 100 days. In the schooling world, it's a single term or 50 school days.

As an external applicant, you must do your homework. Before starting, you should know quite a bit about the school: academic performance, financial position, strategic goals, key performance indicators (KPIs), core workforce issues, market position, student numbers, capital works being planned or in action, and so forth.

You may have met several key staff before you are introduced to the wider community. For a principal appointment, this announcement would come from the board chair or regional director. For a deputy or other senior leadership role, it would come from the principal.

Everyone will have Googled the new guy or gal. They'll have checked out reviews from sites like Rate My Teachers. They'll have looked at the school you've come from. They'll have done a social media check on Facebook and LinkedIn. They may know about your family situation, your qualifications, hobbies, recent visits to sporting venues or museums, maybe even your favourite food. An impression will have been formed before you've even started.

Some friendly advice for 'first time' things

Smile, read the room and be authentic when you first address your staff. Don't try to wow them with data or PowerPoint presentations; just share your humanity. Don't scare them with grandiose plans to change too much immediately; honour and respect their past. Build on the great work of those who came before you, and don't disparage your predecessor. There might be things that very clearly need to be done immediately. There's nothing wrong with highlighting these, and it could actually give you an early win. Share a bit about yourself professionally and personally. Leave some time for Q&A.

Be just as friendly and genuine the first time you address your students. Highlight some of the wonderful things you've heard about them and their accomplishments. There's nothing wrong with noting some areas for improvement, but don't drop into specifics just yet. Be yourself, but project the sort of leadership you feel is needed.

The same goes for your first parental address: be engaging and genuine. Parents will be looking for specifics. This is your opportunity to share your vision and expected standards.

For your first full board meeting, you will usually have to provide a report in a standard format shared with you by the board chair. If no expectations are communicated, use the key priorities listed in the strategic or operational plan as signposts. Depending upon the length of time between your commencement and the first board meeting, a SWOT (strengths, weaknesses, opportunities and threats) analysis might be useful to frame the conversation. Know your own KPIs and those of the school, and understand how you are tracking towards them. You'll likely have a conversation with the board chair prior to the meeting, so you can cover expectations then.

Low-hanging fruit to get you some early wins

- Get to know your people as a priority. If you have a change agenda ahead of you, then you need to build trust and relationships early.
- Build relationships with key groups connected to the school as another priority. Remember the quote attributed to Greek philosopher Epictetus: 'We have two ears and one mouth so that we can listen twice as much as we speak.'
- Gain visibility around the grounds to build your profile and credibility with staff and students. Start to see how students dress, conduct themselves and treat others.
- Decision-making: there's a place for top-down directions, but staff want a leader who considers their opinion, values their feedback and seeks their counsel.
- Communicate in a variety of ways, not all via email.
- Timelines for making changes: try not to do too much too early. Take your time to know what needs to be done, why it needs to be done, who is doing it and when. Remember to acknowledge past achievements.

Internal appointment

As you are already familiar with your organisation, you will be expected to hit the ground running. Often both you and the people whom you now lead will have to make a transition: everyone will still see you as they did in your previous role. The attributes that served you well got you to where you are now, so don't make huge changes. Of course, the expectations of your new role will mean that you can't do all the things you once did. Your mindset may need to move from the operational to the strategic, and you may shift from being the supportive staff mentor to the person who has final responsibility to make the tough calls.

Some pieces of advice and reflection

- Some people are great deputies but for some reason make poor principals. They may find it hard to juggle the additional demands, or to make difficult decisions about the performance issues of staff who were once close colleagues. Before you think about changing the title on your badge, this is something you need to come to grips with.
- People will want to know what sort of leader you will be. If—for instance—you've been a servant leader throughout your career, you aren't likely to change too much. However, the school may need you to adapt your style to implement improvements for the greater good. You need to recognise this and be open to growth.
- There may have been other internal applicants who are now disgruntled. They'll either get over it and get behind you, passive-aggressively undermine you, or eventually leave the school.
- Friendships may be tested, for all the reasons already listed.

Key takeaway

Whether you've just arrived at a school or have been there for a decade, you'll need to prove yourself in a new leadership role. Remember that you got hired for a reason, so prioritise relationships and give people plenty of opportunity to get to know you—as a leader and as a person.

3

Seats on the bus

Lesson #4 *Your school is a bus, and you're driving it. Your first job is to get the seats sorted. Move the right people into those seats. Escort off the bus those who cannot or will not buckle up. Provide good service to the people who buy a ticket to ride.*

In his famous book *Good to Great*, Jim Collins uses a bus analogy as a metaphor for business. Collins believes that it's the job of a leader to get the wrong people off the bus and right people onto the bus and into their correct seats. In my experience, getting the seats sorted ahead of time is the critical first step.

Before actual people are even considered, you must understand the skillset needed for each responsibility. Each bus seat represents a position on your organisational chart. You should consider the line of reporting, level of reporting, level of seniority and level of responsibility that comes with each role. You can take your time organising the seats. This is the easy part: seats don't have feelings. They don't talk back or complain. It's a bit like having a goldfish as a pet!

Everyone in the organisation needs to know who does what and where they can go for answers. How many times have you heard someone say: 'I'm not even sure what he does' or 'Who do I see to get approval for this excursion?' or 'Who do I need to sign off on this purchase?'? A lack of clarity around roles, responsibilities and reporting lines leads to ambiguity, time wastage and confusion.

It is impossible to suggest a universally ideal organisational structure for schools. There are, however, some fundamental rules to follow based on common sense and the core features of schooling. Schools typically have three or four segments: curriculum, pastoral care (including behaviour management and student wellbeing), operations (including administration) and, in larger schools, co-curricular. Each of these segments needs someone in charge, and that someone will have a few people supporting and reporting to them.

Let's look at the curriculum segment of a P–12 school. There will be a head of curriculum, perhaps known as a head of studies, a head of teaching and learning or a deputy principal of academics—these all mean the same bloody thing! Reporting to this person will be one to three deputies, at least one for primary and one for secondary. Reporting to the deputies will be heads of department. In smaller schools there may be subject area co-ordinators with oversight of a few subjects. Then there will be staff responsible for things such as enrichment, learning support and gifted and talented programs. Then of course come the teachers and the teacher aides. Plenty of teachers will report to more than one head of department. Some might teach across primary and secondary, and others might also do learning support. They all need to be represented on an organisational chart somewhere, and that's just one segment of a school! Each of these roles needs to have a position description that reflects their place on the organisational chart.

This is all basic operational stuff, but getting it wrong will lead to frustration, overlap and inefficiencies. If you have the opportunity to organise the seats on the bus, do so. Get them sorted as best you can, then verbally reinforce your decisions with staff at regular intervals. Provide hypothetical scenarios and talk them through, so that everyone can understand who does what and who they go to for decisions or advice.

A leader will naturally tend to think about who is in their team, who is reporting to them, how they intend to lead a particular person or group, and what tasks or responsibilities they have to achieve as a team. It's also vital to think about the team or person to whom you are reporting.

Managing up and managing down

Another one of those things that no-one tells you when you step into a leadership role is that you feel like the meat in a sandwich. As school leaders, we think about and plan for those who report to us, those whom we are meant to serve. However, we ourselves also report to someone—in some cases, to several people. This brings an added layer of stress, because different masters want different things.

Our staff want security, consistency, purpose, support, confidence and appreciation. They want to be well-resourced. They want to have input. They want to know the vision of the school and their place in that vision. They want help in managing students and parents. They want professional learning opportunities.

The people you report to—your principal, your head of school, your regional director, your board chair—want all these things as well. They want their staff to have a sense of purpose and to feel valued. But they also want something more. Their needs are different to those of the people you lead. They want assurance that you can manage all of the things just listed. They also don't want to be burdened with every minor detail. That's your purpose and the reason they employed you.

Managing up as a deputy or middle leader

Beyond the core functions of the leadership role you occupy, your job is to uphold standards, model expectations, drive the implementation of key strategic projects and implement the vision of the principal and the board. To manage up, you will need to provide assurance around and updates on these four areas.

The principal can't be everywhere, so it's up to deputies and middle leaders to be the walking and talking embodiment of school leadership. The principal expects you to solve issues with staff, students and parents and only bring to their attention anything that might pose a bigger risk.

Don't withhold information from the principal. They should have a thick skin and most likely were in a similar role to yours for some time, so they'll have seen it all before. When presenting a problem to a senior leader, it's advisable to come with a proposed solution. You don't need to sugarcoat it.

You're part of a team. If you are a deputy or a head of teaching and learning, then your first team is the senior leadership team of the school. Your second team is the one you lead. In the senior leadership team, you are among equals. As a middle or senior leader, you are flag-bearer, cheerleader and keeper of secrets all in one. Your team must present a united front to the rest of the staff. If there is a fracture, then whatever you are trying to implement will be compromised significantly.

Managing up as principal

Depending upon your relationship with the board, you should ideally be having a meeting or conversation with the chair either weekly or fortnightly. If your school has no board, there is likely to be a commensurate person such as a regional director. At these meetings you will cover a number of operational topics, everything from capital works to recruitment, co-curricular, funding and parental complaints. I'd also discuss student expulsions, extended suspensions, reports to the Department of Child Safety or equivalent, and significant staff welfare and performance issues. There may be some areas, such as WHS or social media, that pose a risk to the school.

Your relationship in these meetings should ideally be collegial, supportive and rapport. Everyone in the room has the best interests of the community at heart, and the board chair or regional director also has a responsibility to help oversee governance, set strategy, manage risk and review policy. They should represent the school community, craft the skillset of board members, build the profile of the school, cultivate external networks and partnerships, contribute to philanthropic activities and mentor the principal.

Key takeaway

Knowing the inner workings of your organisational chart is essential to your success as a leader. With an understanding of each role's individual and interrelated purposes, you'll be able to sort out the seats on the bus before your passengers have even boarded. Enjoy a smooth ride!

4

The power of community

Lesson #5 *A school is strong when the community that surrounds it is strong. Look for ways to build connections, relationships and partnerships. Be deliberate and persistent in this task.*

When you lead a school, you lead a community. Take an average-sized school: 500 students, about 70 staff and a few hundred parents all arrive in the morning and depart in the afternoon. The students and their families live in various parts of the surrounding area. Most of the parents and guardians will have jobs and commitments. Many will hail from countries around the world. Some will be wealthy, some not. There may be Christians, Muslims, atheists, agnostics, Hindus and Buddhists. Some will lean liberal, others conservative. There will be business owners, full-time students, public servants, tradies. Some will be highly educated, others less so. The thing that they all have in common is that their children attend your school.

Parents, staff and students alike need some assurance around a few basic matters. Parents want to know that their child is safe, that they have a few friends, that they are being well educated, and that they are developing some fundamental life skills. Staff want to know that they are valued, that their role has some purpose, that they are appropriately remunerated, and that they have decent working conditions. Students want to feel safe, both physically and psychologically. They want a few friends, they want teachers who like them, and they want to be able to pursue their interests. These people are all part of your community, and you have a responsibility to try and meet all of their needs.

Indicators of a strong school culture

A school is as strong as the community that surrounds it. How do you know when you have a positive culture?

- When you are proud to talk about your school as a parent, student or staff member. Do you hesitate or cringe when you tell someone the name of your school?
- When there are more parents than staff at an information night that has been put on for their benefit. If it's the other way around, then we have a problem.
- When most staff are happy to attend a fun out-of-hours social event. This reveals a culture that makes it enjoyable for colleagues to hang out when not forced to do so, simply because they like each other's company.
- When you do a call-out for volunteers to help at a fete, or for donations towards a winter blanket collection, and you receive plenty of offers from parents.
- When you have a strong community of alumni who stay connected, give back in some way, return to attend events and send their own children to the school.
- When staff and board members send their own children to your school. There might be valid reasons for them not to, but if a good number do so then that's a sign of confidence.
- When there is a healthy attendance of parents at awards ceremonies, presentations and special assemblies.
- When you have an active P&F with at least double figures of attendance at monthly meetings, and when this P&F is actively supporting the school with fundraisers, promotions and event volunteering.

- When a call-out for financial donations to support a family fallen on hard times or to alleviate a wider tragedy is answered in a quick and positive way.
- When there are high numbers of parents attending parent-teacher interviews.
- When you have an active parent-driven WhatsApp group. Now I will admit that these can descend into a forum of negativity. But if no-one has set one up, it's interesting to reflect on that a little. What does it say about parental connectivity? Chat groups are also useful for a different reason: if you can read the comments and have the ability to filter and deflect criticism, they provide a good barometer of feedback. A bit cheeky, I know!

Schools have hugely varying student numbers. Some have boarders. Some have a distance learning component. But if you are reading this, you'll know what a healthy community connection should look like at your own school. I've been at schools where I'd be lucky to get more than 10 parents at a Year 7 parent information night, and another where I couldn't find enough chairs and they were still arriving well after we started.

How to build community connections

School is a place where people seek out connection. Parents do it at sporting carnivals, music events, information nights, volunteer activities and on tuckshop duty. Staff do it in staffrooms and on camps, tours and excursions, and through collaborative planning or simply by sharing a common working space. Students do it throughout the day. Connection is a basic human need. We need to feel part of something we can bond over, something that allows us to share experiences and build friendships.

As a school leader, you need to recognise this and seek out opportunities to facilitate it. A school is strengthened when the community that surrounds it is welcomed, acknowledged, encouraged to be involved and provided with opportunities to engage. Let's explore some targeted ways to build a community.

Food

Feed them and they will come: whether it is a weekend BBQ or a corporate function, people will attend if food is on offer. Events where food is served present an opportunity for you to share important school updates, and are a catalyst for parents to come together to forge friendships and partnerships. This can have a ripple effect across other aspects of school life for years to come.

The arts

Musicals, end-of-year performances, dramatic plays, choirs, art showcases, rock bands—whatever it is, families love to see their children's artistic skills in action. They will flock in droves to be involved with rehearsals or props, take photos or simply enjoy the show.

Sport

It doesn't matter what it is or when it's played: sport brings parents together on weekends, in the afternoon, at training sessions, in the evenings. Dads are cooking BBQs, mums are in the canteen. Some parents are scoring or umpiring, some are just spectating. They're interacting with school staff, and everyone has something in common to talk about.

Awards

Ceremonies where students are acknowledged for their achievements always bring communities together. Award distribution typically occurs at special assemblies or at the end of the term, the semester or the year. These events also provide a chance for the principal, the board chair or the head of teaching and learning to share the latest initiatives. Add some food and you've hit the sweet spot.

Special days

These include significant occasions such as Mother's Day and Father's Day. Plenty of schools do Grandparents' Day as well. ANZAC Day and Remembrance Day can also be added to this list. Depending on your school's religious affiliation, you may have other significant dates to draw people together in ceremony.

Special events

There are a few major celebrations that can bring community together. The school fete is a big one, possibly the biggest of them all. Book week has become huge, especially the book character parade. Science week and Under Eights week are other opportunities. Sporting carnivals where the whole school is involved are also wonderful—especially if you add a BBQ, a coffee van and a fundraiser. Triple threat right there!

Fundraisers

Typical fundraising events are now more than just Bunnings-style sausage sizzles. You may find yourself hosting golf days, cocktail parties and lunches featuring sports stars. These events often have guest speakers and can raise significant coin, but they are also great bonding events for parents and staff.

Service

Service activities are a great way to bring people together. Plenty of schools build these events into their pastoral care programs as a way to instil in their students a sense of humility, justice, generosity and empathy. Activities may include:

- Providing meals to homeless folks in partnership with a local church or charity
- Collecting and distributing blankets and non-perishable food during the winter months
- Helping impoverished people in other parts of the world to build wells, hospitals, schools and accommodation
- Visiting aged-care facilities
- Engaging in yearly activities such as Clean Up Australia Day
- Collecting money to alleviate specific environmental catastrophes

Allied health

Schools provide a perfect space to house allied health professionals for the benefit of students and even staff. Services may be offered on a short- or long-term basis and include vaccinations, dental care, eyesight testing and hearing testing.

Parent support groups

In addition to the P&F, parents may care to join supporter groups for a sport or an activity. Disclaimer: it only takes one rogue parent who is involved for all the wrong reasons to turn other parents off and make the group into a nightmare for a principal. But don't be dissuaded! A core group of kind-hearted wonderful parents can build significant capital among the wider parent community.

Social media

Facebook and WhatsApp are common platforms. Parents will often set one up for their child's own grade or class. These groups are a great way to share, reach out, ask questions, send reminders and acknowledge others.

Key takeaway

I recommend that all leaders use a list like the one above to audit their school for community connection. If you tick off at least one item per term, you'll have a variety of opportunities to build strong relationships. Take a look at the past year to see how many events your school held, then look to the year or the semester ahead. How and when can you build these items into your school calendar? You will soon discover the unparalleled multiplier effect that a strong community connection has on the academic, social and emotional development of the entire student cohort.

5
The purpose of a vision

Lesson #6 *A vision is the ultimate aspirational goal for your school, the foundation upon which everything else is built. Alignment with the classroom is critical: you don't want your vision to be a bunch of nebulous flowery words that nobody buys into.*

Ambitious, audacious and somewhat idealistic, a vision aims to transform lives for the better. Creating a vision for a school is a truly tricky thing. A vision makes a public statement about the school's view on the purpose of education and how students should learn. It has to be the collective aspiration of all members of the school community.

Good principals will seek the input of staff, students and parents by running surveys, leading focus groups and organising forums. They'll seek feedback from the board and from the broader community. Doing this groundwork serves a few purposes: it informs strategic planning, it gives everyone a voice and it forms partnerships by bringing people together.

The board should certainly have its own vision for the school, as will the Department of Education and the school system. But it is ultimately the role of the principal to establish a vision for their school community.

From the vision emerges the strategic plan. From the strategic plan emerges the operational plan. From the operational plan emerge specific goals, and from these goals KPIs are established. The principal needs to drive all of this. You should be able to point to the vision to tell people the reasoning behind your choices for the school.

Bringing a vision to life

So you've created a vision and a strategy to achieve it with the requisite goals, responsibilities and timeframes. All up, it has probably taken three to six months. It will be broadcast to the school community with a bit of fanfare—at the very least a group email and a blurb in the newsletter. That's the easy part. The hard part is bringing the bloody thing to life. This is another reason why you have to get those seats on the bus sorted first.

As I've said, every school needs to make a public statement on the purpose of education and how students should learn. This will usually be done through a vision statement, often with an accompanying mission statement. Sometimes a school will list the mission statement before the vision statement, sometimes the two will be combined to create a single statement, sometimes there is a thing called a purpose statement and sometimes there is a thing called a values statement. Honestly, no wonder most people see it all as just a lot of waffle!

It is absolutely critical, however, for a school community—led by the principal—to define who they are, what they want to create and how they will create it. A school has to put a stake in the ground and proudly say to the world 'this is what we stand for'. Everything flows from a school's vision and mission statements, so all needs to be in alignment: values, strategy, priorities, goals, actions, KPIs. This alignment should affect decision-making, hiring practices, school events and celebrations, and ultimately the climate and culture of the organisation.

Vision statements and mission statements

A vision statement declares what a school wants to be, while a mission statement shows what action will be taken to get there.

Vision statements

- Outline a school's objectives or goals
- Are future-oriented declarations of the school's purpose and aspirations
- Are clear and unambiguous
- Paint a bright and compelling picture
- Use memorable and engaging language
- Have realistic and achievable ambitions
- Align with values and culture
- Are sources of motivation

Vision statements answer the following questions:

- What do we want to do?
- When do we want to do it?
- How do we want to do it?

Mission statements

- Indicate how the school aims to achieve its vision
- Communicate the school's reason for being, and how it aims to serve its key stakeholders
- Concentrate on the present, describing what a school wants to do now

Mission statements answer the following questions:

- What does your school do today?
- Who are you doing it for?
- What is the benefit?
- What is the purpose and what are the values of your school?
- Who are your primary stakeholders?
- What are your responsibilities towards these people?
- What are the main objectives that support the school in accomplishing its mission?

Vision and mission statements should be dynamic, clearly articulated and evocative while inspiring action and support. Here's an example:

> *Our vision is to empower students to acquire, demonstrate and value knowledge and skills that will support them, as life-long learners, to participate in and contribute to the global world and practise the core values of the school: respect, inclusion and excellence.*
>
> *Our mission is to enable access to learning for all students through the provision of:*
>
> - *Differentiated, in-depth and cohesive learning programs aligned to year-level content and achievement standards informed by the Australian Curriculum*
> - *Highly effective teachers focused on improving student outcomes through their commitment to ongoing professional development, quality teaching, evidence-based practices, coaching, mentoring and collaboration*
> - *A high-quality inclusive learning environment that is responsive to student voice*

From vision to action

So how do you transform your vision into reality? You've going to need a plan, some goals in mind to achieve that plan, some actions to achieve those goals, and some way of measuring your progress. It needs to look something like this:

1. *Vision*—sometimes a purpose statement is included before a vision to provide an organisation's reason for being, but for a school this should be self-evident.
2. *Mission*—a tagline may be included to accompany the mission and vision. This is a slick marketing one-liner that captures the essence of the school: 'Let your light shine', 'Learning to learn', 'Learning today, leading tomorrow'.
3. *Values*—usually covering key items such as respect, compassion, excellence and integrity. Every school in the country has its own clearly articulated set of values.

4. *Strategy or strategic plan*—brings the vision to life with priorities and key goals for five or six key areas of a school, typically across a three-year timeline.
5. *Operational plan*—usually a one-year slice of the strategic plan, but with a lot more detail including goals, objectives, action items, names and dates. This is where you lay out the practical, measurable, actionable tasks that bring the vision to fruition.
6. *Goals and objectives*—each key area or priority within the strategic and operational plans needs to have approximately four to six goals and objectives that will allow you to realise your ambitions for the school.
7. *Action items*—a goal is a target, and an action item explains how you will attain it. There might be a few action items for each goal.
8. *KPIs*—these enable you to track and measure performance or progress towards the achievement of a goal or key priority.

Building an operational plan

The following table demonstrates a small piece of a typical operational plan, focusing on the strategic priority area of students. There are three goals for this area and a series of actions to achieve each goal. Attached to each action is a timeframe and a person responsible for getting it done. You'll notice some colours on the far right—that's a classic traffic-light approach to indicate progress. Green means complete, blue means progressing well and red means slow progress.

This is a real portion of the operational plan that I have used in the past and continue to use today. It may not appeal to everyone, but it doesn't need to. What matters is that you have a plan with goals, timelines and clear delegation.

Our students	Actions to achieve this goal	Timeframe	Who is responsible?	Current Progress	Comment
Goal 1 Support the academic, social and emotional wellbeing of all students	Investigate and select a program, share details with staff and wider community. Explore Positive Schools, positive psychology, PERMA and character strengths.	T3 2022			Staff will attend workshops in T4 2022
	Conduct a student survey to inform how we may support the social and emotional wellbeing of students, and to give us general baseline data.	T4 2022			Surveys being done in T4
	Create an implementation plan that includes regular reviews and adjustments: what, how, when, who, why. Map out our school-wide social and emotional wellbeing program for students.	T4 2022			We met in T2 for a workshop that mapped out the next 6 months
	Build staff capacity to deliver the social and emotional program and broader support.	T1 2023 and ongoing			Purchased Second Steps
	Academic Care: ensure that staff use this time to assist students. Staff must know their students very well. They need to monitor progress and intervene where necessary. Students must be provided with necessary skills.	T1 2022			Absorbed into the WISE program
	Establish an authentic life-skills program that is practical and engaging.	T1 2022			This has been absorbed into the WISE program and planning has commenced

Our students	Actions to achieve this goal	Timeframe	Who is responsible?	Current Progress	Comment
Goal 2 Provide a range of co-curricular opportunities for sport, music, art and activities	Establish a co-curricular plan that considers sport, outdoor education, the arts, pastoral care and service learning.	T4 2021 & T1 2022			Going well
	Introduce staff to these opportunities and explore ways to enter teams into local competitions, to enable group performances or to display student talents.	T4 2021 & T1 2022			Ongoing, going well
	Establish a yearly MAD (music, art, drama) event to showcase skills.	T3 2022			T4 2022–with EOYP Continue to combine with EOYP
	Provide district sport pathways and programs for the whole school. Partner with local schools to create a small competition.	Ongoing			
	This program needs to link to our overall wellbeing, leadership and behaviour frameworks.	T1 2023			
Goal 3 Establish a Student Leadership Program	Establish our student leadership organisational chart with clear positions and responsibilities.	T1 2022			SRC has started
	Create an operations handbook for all student leaders to guide actions and practices, to provide student committees with direction, and to lead the application process.	T3 2022			
	Embed leadership opportunities into camp programs, service learning and behaviour framework.	Ongoing			
	Establish a mentoring program as part of our leadership and service programs, in particular for younger students and new students.	T2 2022			Yr 11/7 mentor program started
	Explore ways in which we can partner to build leadership with universities, workplaces, guest presenters, charities etc.	T1 2023			

Key takeaway

A vision isn't simply an abstract statement—it needs to align with strategy and be evident in everyday behaviours. Your school's vision should guide each operational goal that you put into action. A vision statement can be complemented by a purposeful mission statement that indicates how the school will realise its aspirations. If you meaningfully involve the school community in the delivery of your vision and mission, you will be well on your way to success.

6
The importance of visibility

Lesson #7 Get comfortable with being visible. Visibility does more than put a face to a name—it builds your understanding of the organisation and everyone else's trust in you.

Every interaction at school is an opportunity to strengthen your relationships, build your profile, share information and learn about others. Make an effort to get out from behind your desk every day or every second day. Put time aside every week to catch up with someone in the organisation. Do this just twice per week and that's about 80 people you're catching up with in a single year! Include visibility-building time in your calendar and work around it.

As I've been banging on about throughout this book, there are three groups of people in any school: staff, students and parents. Each will need to see you and interact with you regularly. You can do this in a number of ways, as long as you're consistent. I recommend that you try for some daily interaction with each group.

You don't have to be an extrovert: introverts can make great school leaders. But get comfortable with being seen. Present in front of groups, speak to people instead of emailing them and come out from behind your laptop. Just as teachers should be active and mobile in the classroom, leaders should be active and mobile around the school.

What visibility does

Staff reassurance

To staff, your presence conveys reliability and order. There's nothing better for an early-career teacher than to see the experienced deputy or principal walking the halls and verandas. They feel that someone has their back—especially if they have a tough class.

Students on notice

Students are more mindful of their actions and less likely to misbehave if they see you, or know that you are likely to be walking around the corner at any moment.

Role-modelling

You need to model your expectations of cleanliness, uniform and conduct. What you walk past becomes your standard.

Rapport

Moving around campus means building relationships: acknowledging, reminding, checking in, learning names, hearing about people's lives, solving problems. It's impossible to measure the impact of these everyday interactions.

Trust

You will build a level of trust and integrity with staff if you are regularly visible. Seeing you out and about in classrooms and the playground tells them that you are in the trenches with them.

Temperature check

You can gauge people's energy levels, see who is struggling, pick up on patterns of behaviour and work out where the risk areas are.

Parent reassurance

Parents want to know that they're dropping off their child into safe hands. Being present at the school gate allows you to chat with them and improve relationships. You will build your profile and enable people to put a face to the name that they see in newsletters, social media posts, reports and letters.

Key moments for building visibility

Morning tea and lunchtime

These break times are your chance to see as many people as possible, and for them to see you. Visit staffrooms and mingle with students in the playground. Address uniform infringements and silly behaviour to prevent escalation.

Pick-up & drop-off

Be a regular presence in the car park. Help with supervision. Help with traffic flow. Greet students and parents as they arrive, and farewell them as they depart. Try to do this once per week. Over the course of a school year, you'll have notched up 40 visits.

Events

Events are a great opportunity to build relationships with small talk. Importantly, they are your main opportunity to see lots of parents. There are plenty of parents—usually dads—who only turn up to a rugby game on a Saturday. You won't make it to every school event, but mark them all in your calendar and try your best to attend. The students will enjoy your support, and so too will staff.

Put your own stuff last

If you teach, your lesson will be the last thing you prepare. The needs of your staff come before your own, so prepare well and prepare early. You'll need to be an accomplished teacher in your own right in order to juggle everything.

Talk at assemblies and staff meetings

It doesn't need to be a long monologue—you simply have to get up and talk. This is a chance to acknowledge and celebrate an achievement, team or person. It's a chance to reinforce expectations or to remind people about an upcoming event. Treat every assembly and staff meeting as an opportunity to establish culture.

Staffrooms

Join your colleagues for lunch on a regular basis. You might have a few different staffrooms to rotate yourself around. Visit in the morning to meet and greet, and put on breakfasts or morning tea to create conversation and bonding.

Small talk

Get comfortable with small talk. The best way to initiate a conversation is to ask someone about themselves, their family, their hobby, their weekend or their holiday plans.

Video

Plenty of school leaders now produce short, punchy video updates. These often function as a replacement for the newsletter. Most of your parents will be connected to Facebook, Instagram or LinkedIn. Let them see and hear you.

Key takeaway

Leading a school doesn't mean that you need to have the loudest voice. It doesn't mean that you need to be the stereotypically charismatic, transformational, verbose leader. Your visibility is more important than any of this. Wake up, get up, lace up and show up every day.

7

Difficult conversations

Lesson #8 No-one likes to have difficult conversations, but avoiding them means endorsing bad behaviour, killing morale, lowering standards and losing good people.

In my experience, the most challenging experiences for a school leader are those times when you must initiate conversations about staff performance and conduct. On these occasions, and there have been plenty, I've found the discussions confronting and often unpleasant in parts. Along the way, I've also discovered a few tricks to make them easier. That is the focus of this chapter.

What makes a conversation difficult?

Difficult conversations are emotional conversations. That's right, that gooey stuff called feelings! When feelings are involved, things become complicated. There are subtleties in identifying the type of conversation that would be classified as difficult. Typically, it will revolve around issues affecting the performance, conduct or wellbeing of staff members. The difficulty lies in the potential of the topic to embarrass the person by calling into question their ability or integrity. Reactions may range from shame to anger to acceptance. Consider whether the conversation will be deflating to the person and adversely affect their self-confidence. Will it have a negative impact on staff culture, climate or harmony? These factors shouldn't stop you from having a difficult conversation, but they might shape your approach. Remember that these conversations can have ripple effects that may cause you drama later. Nonetheless, avoiding the situation because you are worried about the consequences is not a suitable option.

Levels of difficulty

Here are real-world scenarios from my own experience to illustrate the issues that may warrant a difficult conversation.

Level 1: Low

Perhaps you have a colleague who is constantly turning up late to staff meetings. Perhaps they have trouble submitting their academic reports on time. Perhaps they're not addressing kids about their poor uniform. It's these little things that can erode a culture. This might just require a quick corridor conversation, no appointment or call into the principal's office needed. It doesn't need to be formally documented. Don't send a follow-up email, but make a note in your diary just in case it does escalate.

Level 2: Medium

Are you receiving complaints from a parent about the lack of support, care or quality instruction given to their child by a specific teacher? This would warrant a private conversation with or without a support person. It will require a follow-up email and a post-meeting check-in. A plan needs to be put in place to rectify the issue, and you should personally send an update to the parent concerned.

Level 3: High

This is potential performance-management territory. A Level 3 conversation can be merited by allegations of workplace bullying or harassment. It can also be the result of unsuccessful Level 1 and Level 2 conversations. The outcome of this conversation might be a formal warning or a performance improvement plan. Level 3 requires a formal meeting, a support person and a follow-up email or letter with clear expectations and outcomes.

What can you do to support yourself?

Level 1 and Level 2 conversations might be within your realm of comfort, and you won't lose any sleep over them. Level 3, though, can be particularly draining. Dealing with multiple Level 1s and 2s on a weekly basis will also take a toll on you emotionally. You have to look after yourself and recognise the signs of stress. Don't do as I did and seek relaxation by hitting the bottle. Debrief with a colleague, the board chair or an external mentor. Find some joy in another part of school life to remind yourself of your reasons for doing this job, and refer to Chapter 9 for useful self-care tips!

Strategies for difficult conversations

If you wear a badge that says principal or deputy or head of something, then you have a responsibility to have difficult conversations when the time comes. The worst thing you can do is to ignore the issue, hope that it will disappear over time or kick the can up the food chain for someone else to deal with. Choosing to confront the issue shows that you have a bit of grit and integrity. You will send the message that you're willing to tackle something for the greater good of the organisation. People want this in their leader. They don't want a pushover.

The immediacy effect

The time you spend thinking about how you should approach a conversation is excruciating. Once it's over, you will wonder why you didn't do it earlier. Every day that you wait to have the chat makes it harder to address. Once an issue that warrants a conversation has been identified, the immediacy effect kicks in straight away. Get it done as early as possible.

You need a plan

Don't go into a difficult conversation without a plan. You need to write down the issues to be discussed, the impact they are having and what needs to be done about them. I don't mean that you should already have your mind made up. A difficult conversation doesn't need to be combative. If it is, the opportunity for growth and improvement is probably lost. It helps to know what sort of person you are about to have a conversation with. What sort of relationship do you already have with them? Have you had conversations of the challenging kind already? Is this person generally receptive to feedback, or does the fight part of the fight or flight response kick in quickly? Having answers to these questions will help you formulate your pre-game plan.

Shine a light on the problem, not the person

If a person stands any chance of improving, then their behaviour needs to be redeemable. If you target the person instead of the problem, you imply that the issue resides somewhere deep inside their character and goes to the heart of who they are. Stay away from character assassination and focus on resolution. The person needs to first recognise that there is a problem. They can then provide some potential solutions—the preferable first course of action—or you can offer them up yourself.

Keep your cool

Some people are masters at turning a situation around, making it your problem and suggesting that they haven't been supported. If they put as much thought into what they were supposed to be doing, these conversations wouldn't be needed! As much as you'd like to go all Mike Tyson on them, remember that you are in a leadership position because someone at some point thought you'd be calm under pressure. If you lose your cool, you've lost the conversation and any chance of finding a suitable resolution.

Avoid the rabbit hole

Don't get sidetracked. Some people are great at not really hearing what the issue is, but instead will divert the conversation to something completely unrelated. One minute you're talking about an abject lack of planning and the next you're discussing the apparent lack of suitable whiteboard pens that is affecting their ability to teach effectively. Suddenly it's your fault again! Clever, but don't fall for it. Keep redirecting them back to the topic.

Three: the magic number

Have a few points to discuss. If you have a list of 10, then you've clearly let things fester. Pick the worst three and run with those. More than three issues can become a tad overwhelming for the person, and difficult for them to realistically address. A long list also indicates that things may have moved beyond a conversation into the formal realm of performance improvement.

A support person

Not all difficult conversations require a support person. Feel free to offer this option to someone if you think a friendly presence might reduce tension or anxiety. Sometimes the support person will advocate for you just as much as they will for the other person. Be warned: a support person can occasionally be argumentative and make things worse, even though they shouldn't be saying much at all. Stick to your plan.

Commit to paper

Follow up with a written summary of what was discussed:

a. These were the concerns
b. This is what we discussed
c. This is what we agreed
d. This is how I will support you

This consolidates the conversation and gives it some legitimacy. It also ensures a lack of ambiguity and allows the person to reflect on the conversation once the emotion has subsided. Should the issue arise again sometime later, you will have a written history of evidence to draw upon.

Check in

Schedule a little check-in for a day or two after the meeting. This part of the process can be formal or informal, and is intended to encourage accountability. It tells the person that they are being monitored, that the issue raised is important and that you want to see a change.

Key takeaway

Difficult conversations are the least enjoyable part of leadership, but potentially the most important. No-one wants to have them, but they come with the territory. With careful thought you can make them at least tolerable, effective and sustaining. I hope this chapter has provided some useful insights into strategies for managing difficult conversations. When done well, they will have a significant impact on organisational effectiveness.

8

Building your team

Lesson #9 *Build your team with mutual respect and clear expectations, and allow them to do the same with their teams. It's one of the most powerful ways to achieve your collective organisational goals.*

Think back on your life and the teams that you've been part of—sporting teams, project teams, music groups, drama groups. Teams are so much more enjoyable and productive when everyone gets along, when each person knows their role, when there are no egos, agendas, undermining attempts or put-downs. In a good team, individuals act in the best interests of the collective. No peanuts, muppets or pelicans!

Maybe you're joining an established team at a new school or have been elevated into a team-leading position. Maybe you've been lucky enough to create your own team. Whatever the scenario relevant to you, the following reflections and advice will be applicable.

Foolproof strategies

Know who is on your team

Of course you know who is on your team, but how well do you really know them? Their gifts, their weaknesses, their work preferences, their learning styles, their communication styles, their levels of experience? How about—staying within the bounds of personal comfort, without getting too personal—their family, interests or hobbies? Leading a team of people is not dissimilar to teaching a class of students. Building rapport and relationships with your teammates will allow the achievement of tasks to be so much more efficient and successful.

Build individual and collective capacity

We've all heard the sayings *you're only as strong as your weakest link* and *a rising tide lifts all boats*. If you build the capacity of each individual, everyone benefits. By enhancing the collective capacity of your team, you enhance enjoyment and fulfilment while increasing your chances of success.

Establish a few team expectations

These are the largely unwritten rules around how members of a group should engage with each other to make decisions. Your expectations may have to do with communication, attendance at events, contribution to meetings, the actioning of agenda items and the maintenance of a united team front. At every one of my senior leadership team meetings, for instance, I check in on everyone's wellbeing before we get into the agenda items. At those same meetings, personal opinions are put aside and collaborative effort begins once a group decision has been made.

Use multiple lines of communication

Here are four methods of communication that I use for different purposes with my team.

WhatsApp—Informal chatting, sharing, quick turnaround.

Email—More formal and detailed, to be used when instructions and feedback are required, slower turnaround.

Face-to-face meetings and briefings—To share information, to debate a topic or make a group decision, to acknowledge and celebrate.

Microsoft Teams—To collaborate, to save and store documents for later use.

Be vulnerable, admit mistakes and ask for help

You don't need to know it all, solve it all or lead it all. It's impossible. You will make mistakes and you will inadvertently upset people. You will feel overwhelmed and you will need help. The earlier you recognise this the better.

You'll win the respect and admiration of those on your team if you're okay with vulnerability, admit when you've made a mistake and ask for help when you need it. The old model of leadership doesn't gel in today's workplace, and it's simply not healthy for you. As well as competence and capability, you need to show a little humility, understanding and kindness.

Maintain cabinet solidarity

When your team comes together in a meeting, a number of decisions will be made in the best interests of the school. Not everyone may agree with these decisions, and there may be heated debate. Nothing, however, erodes trust and integrity more than someone breaking rank and disparaging their teammates to other members of staff. Not only is it damaging to the team, but it's perhaps the most effective way to undermine a leader. A lack of solidarity can cause dissent, disharmony and fracturing across an entire school staff. Decisions should be backed publicly at all times by the team and with other members of staff. Whatever is said behind closed doors stays behind closed doors. As soon as they open, you must put on a united front. Any leak in the team must be addressed, because it will undermine everything that you do.

Have a laugh

One thing that has served me well as a leader over the years is a healthy sense of humour. Being able to laugh—whether at yourself or with your team—is important. There will be plenty of tense moments and tough conversations, so your ability to bring a smile to someone's face is most welcome and needed.

The ability to inject humour is useful for other reasons. It breaks the ice in awkward situations. It starts conversations. It gives people permission to relax. It signals friendship.

Make a plan and implement it

Is your team just floating along the school year, doing what it needs to do but not really on fire or reaching great heights? Everything is a bit average? No-one is out of their comfort zone?

Perhaps you all come together every week or fortnight to tick off action items, but without targets or measures of success. There is confusion around roles, and things aren't actioned because no-one is sure whose job that really is. Everything has a sense of mediocrity. The same issues keep popping up and are never resolved. Poor performance is not addressed, and neither is dissatisfaction. There is an underlying sense of passive agitation between some members of the team.

These are signs that a team is leaderless and ineffectual, or at least not as effective as it could be. Things need to be resolved and a plan needs to be put in place. That plan should have clear purpose, targets and measures. It will lead to improved performance and fulfilment. It will contribute to better outcomes for colleagues, students and parents.

As the well-worn proverb says: *If you want to go fast, go alone. If you want to go far, go together.* My experience with school leadership is that I can go faster *and* further with others. There are simply so many things to accomplish at a school at any given time that the power of a well-functioning team is unbeatable. A great team will allow you to achieve your goals, share in the success of others, build staff capacity and see your students succeed.

Coaching and mentoring

As a team leader, you should be doing more than setting goals and bringing everyone together to get tasks done. Your role is to develop the skills, capacity and confidence of those in your team. This is where coaching and mentoring come in handy.

What's the difference between the two? A coach will help someone find their own answers by asking the right questions. A mentor will directly provide the answers to someone less experienced. Coaching and mentoring will empower your team members to work and solve problems independently without you doing all the heavy lifting. They're also a great way to develop the ability of less experienced people to take on leadership roles one day. Think of it as succession planning.

There are a few things to consider when it comes to coaching models. I've enjoyed using the GROW (Goal, Reality, Obstacles/Options, Way Forward) model introduced in Sir John Whitmore's *Coaching for Performance*. The framework provided by Michael Bungay Stanier in *The Coaching Habit* is also useful, especially for those moments when a brief conversation is all you have time for. Observing and modelling classroom practice through instructional coaching is another methodology that you may wish to consider. Whatever framework you choose, it is doomed to failure if you aren't intentional with your coaching. Learn at least the basics of coaching and set aside time for the process. Invest in it and encourage others to do the same.

Key takeaway

Your team is your biggest asset. Invest wisely and you will see great returns. By demonstrating that you value each individual's strengths and contributions, you will build a collective spirit of confidence and trust. If you see room for improvement, take the lead in developing your team's capacity through coaching and mentoring.

9

Self-care: Slay the beast and avoid burnout

Lesson #10 *Self-care is a regular meeting with yourself that might just save not only your health, but also your career, your family and your life.*

It took me about eight years of principalship to start focusing on my physical and psychological health. Until that moment I had allowed the demands of staff, parents, students and the board to take priority. This almost cost me everything.

Although I loved leading a school community, I look back on those years and see that I relied on coping mechanisms like alcohol to relax. I gradually fell into a negative cycle of drinking, weight gain, depression and more drinking. I wasn't a binge drinker and I didn't miss any work commitments. But it certainly didn't ensure that I was operating at peak performance.

The life of a school leader is not always conducive to healthy practices. You face long hours and lots of sitting down in meetings. There are always sausage sizzles, breakfasts, fundraising galas and community events. It's all too easy to get into the habit of working extended hours that don't leave enough time for life. If that's happened to you, you're probably not exercising or eating right. The demands of school leadership will never abate and the hours of work will continue to be long. So what can you do?

I won't simply say that any of the following practices are an instant fix. If it were that easy, we'd all be living in a blissful state of relaxation with a body fat percentage in single figures. But there are real, practical things you can do to start turning your life back around.

Self-care practices that work

Movement

I'm purposefully saying movement instead of exercise, because the latter has connotations of gruelling sessions in the gym. There's nothing wrong with that! But it's important that you move your body in a way that you can sustain and find enjoyable. This doesn't mean moving from office to car to couch. It means raising a mild sweat and elevating the heart rate. You'll feel better, think better, sleep better, work better.

An active meeting with yourself

Schedule morning movement as your first meeting of the day. If mornings aren't an option because your household teeters on the verge of anarchy once the children wake up, then the afternoon may be a better option. Either way, make it regular and consistent. Hold this meeting three times per week for a minimum of 45 minutes. Put it in your calendar if you need to.

Do meal prep on Sunday and eat breakfast every day

If you're ironing your clothes for the week on Sunday, you may as well do meal prep too. Grab five plastic containers for Monday to Friday. Cook up some healthy food, portion it and chuck it in the fridge. Every weekday morning you can simply grab your pre-prepared container, add a yoghurt, banana or muesli bar and off you go. You must also eat breakfast. It fills you, it fuels you, it kick-starts your metabolism. It doesn't have to be much. Sometimes a healthy smoothie will do the trick. Just limit the bacon and pastry options.

Have one cheat day per week

If you enjoy a beer, a wine, a chocolate or an ice-cream, then pick a day to indulge. No point going cold turkey unless you plan on entering a bodybuilding competition in 12 weeks. Use your cheat day as a reward.

Maintain friendships outside of work

Friends on the other side of the fence keep you grounded and give you a chance to talk about non-school stuff. You can drop the badge and just be you.

Sleep

If you are getting up at 5am every morning, then 10pm needs to be your shut-eye time. At least seven hours per night should be your goal. A lack of sleep is like drunkenness; it impairs everything.

Enjoy your hobbies

Find that fun activity that has nothing to do with work, that little piece of bliss that gives you joy.

Break your week up

If you are doing long hours with plenty of evening or weekend commitments, then think about an early finish or a late start one or two days per week. Give yourself permission to start at 10am or clock off at 1pm to get to the gym, play some golf, go for a ride or have a late breakfast with the family. One of the highlights of my week is a Friday morning breakfast out with my boys.

Find a mentor or coach

Or at least a critical friend to catch up with over a coffee!

Remember that you're not irreplaceable

Teachers and school leaders pride ourselves on doing a fabulous job and work ourselves to the bone not to let people down. If you were to disappear one day, your school would roll on and quickly replace you. Your family, however, would miss you terribly. So look after yourself, spend time with your loved ones and prioritise your wellbeing.

Cherish your family

As school leaders, we always attend important events for other children. Sometimes, though, it's nice to attend an event that's important to our own children: a first day at a new school, a graduation, a special assembly, an awards ceremony. These don't come around that often, and you can't go back and do them again later. Invest time in your family. You, your spouse and your children will all be the better for it. Put time aside, turn off your phone and close your laptop. It will all be there when you come back.

Explore ikigai

What is a purpose that brings you joy and satisfaction? Ikigai is the Japanese secret to a long and happy life. It refers to that sweet spot between what you love to do, what you are good at, what the world needs and what you can be paid for. Find your ikigai and pursue it.

You don't need to be at every event

As a senior leader, you will have other leaders in your team to call upon. There will be some events that you simply need to attend, but don't be afraid to otherwise invite someone else to go as your proxy or simply as a representative of the leadership team.

Take responsibility for your growth and development

By the time you reach a senior leadership role in a school, you will have learnt enough about yourself and received enough feedback to see which areas you need some professional learning in.

Get away from it all

Early in my career when I had some time away from school, I found that I would end up doing work whenever I stayed home for the school holidays. Admittedly I loved it, but the lack of breaks would accumulate to the point where I'd sometimes hit a wall at the back end of a term. It was always too easy to open the laptop to do some planning or some research for an upcoming workshop. Even if it's only for a few days, try and get away from it all by going camping, or glamping, or travelling somewhere affordable with the family or even by yourself.

Build your team and delegate

You can't do it all, and you have a responsibility to develop others in your team to one day take over from you or contribute to the profession elsewhere. Put effort into developing the skillsets of others in your department, sub-school or senior leadership team.

Let it go

You can't solve it all, and you don't want to be a martyr. If you can't find a solution to a problem, you must either accept a best fit or jettison it and move on. At some point you need to decide how much time and energy you can use up in hope of a favourable outcome. It may be best to cut your losses and move on, concentrating instead on something that will make a difference.

Make decisions for the right reasons

As difficult as some decisions may be, and as difficult as some consequences may be, you can sleep soundly at night if you've done things the right way. Have you taken into consideration all variables? Is it in the best interests of the organisation? Have you treated those affected with kindness and respect?

Replace a bad habit with a good one

Regular indulgences—perhaps a drink every night after work—will accumulate, and an unhelpful habit needs to be replaced by something if you want to sustain the change. It also helps to pre-plan. If you know you'll reach for the wine in the evening, then make sure to have plenty of healthier substitutes available.

Try the following replacements:

Alcohol with a sugar-free soft drink...

A cigarette or a vape with a coffee or a tea...

Chocolate with a piece of fruit...

Stress eating with a walk or a chat...

Forgive yourself

Maybe in the past you've made on-the-run decisions that you'd now do differently. Maybe you've said things without thinking them through, and would gladly hit the rewind button. Maybe you've admonished a student or a colleague in front of others and have seen them wilt before your eyes. You've lost a bit of respect and you can't stop kicking yourself for it. Guess what? You're human. You've made mistakes and you'll continue to make them. Own them where you can, acknowledge them where you can, fix them where you can, say sorry where you can, but most importantly forgive yourself.

Set yourself a big, fat, hairy (BFH) goal outside of work

It enables you to focus on something that's not work-related. It gives you a sense of fulfilment. It allows your mind to have a break. It gets you out of your comfort zone and makes you feel truly alive.

Believe in yourself

If they're well thought-out, your decisions are ones that anyone in your role would and should make. Maybe you inherited a role where actions should've been taken but weren't, so now they have fallen to you. This is why you are in the role.

Find your school joy

You became a teacher for a reason, and you've stayed in the profession for a reason. We all have a part of school life that lights us up, that reminds us why we chose education as a career and gives us energy. Go back to that when you need it.

Use your gatekeepers

Gatekeepers are those staff who can intercept people, phone calls, emails and walk-ins. I don't mean that they should completely insulate you, but they can do three things to make your life easier: spread the burden, redirect issues and solve problems.

Don't neglect your health check-ups

As we get older, things start to happen to our bodies. We need regular maintenance. Don't postpone or ignore these big ones: skin, bowel, prostate, mammograms, pap smears, eyesight, cholesterol. They might just save your life!

Key takeaway

The best leader you can be is a leader who is healthy and positive with a decent work-life balance. It's true that school can get the best of us at times, and there may be periods where you seem to spend all your waking hours working. Even when it seems impossible, taking time for yourself isn't an optional extra—it's essential if you want to be the role model that your school community needs.

10

Resource management: Things that open and shut

Lesson #11 *As dull as it might sound, resource management is a critical part of school leadership. People don't notice when it's working, but they sure as hell do when it isn't. When not done well, it can bring a school to its knees.*

So you've moved up the ranks of school leadership because you have some ability in teaching, public speaking, curriculum design and managing large groups of students. It appears that you get along with most of your colleagues, you can hold a conversation and you can manage your emotions under pressure. You can juggle quite a few tasks at once, and you can pull off an event with some degree of success. Overall, you are a competent and capable individual with a bit of ambition and drive. As a result of this, you find yourself in a role that also requires you to manage the non-human aspects of school life—everything that opens and shuts and costs something. Budgets, buildings, books, equipment, facilities, resources and spaces: these things have an impact on staff, students and parents.

So what is resource management?

When we hear the phrase 'resource management', it doesn't fill our hearts and minds with a great deal of excitement. You won't see it listed as a core area of leadership in any textbook or leadership guru's LinkedIn post. It's not glamorous or sexy, it won't get you promoted, it may not even get you noticed. But it is an absolutely critical area of school life. If you aspire to leadership or are currently in a leadership role, then you'd better get your head around the fact that you need to manage and provide leadership in this space. Resource management is not the sole responsibility of the business manager or the head of operations. It is the responsibility of the entire school leadership team, with the principal having ultimate sign-off.

Schools are expensive places to operate and complex machines to manage. Public schools receive most of their funding from the state government, and may have a small income stream from levies for laptops, camps and excursions. Independent schools receive funding from a few sources. The federal government provides the majority of it and the state government also provides a significant income stream. Tuition fees, building grants, philanthropic avenues and levies are additional sources of revenue. Every year, these funds need to be allocated across all aspects of school operations and spent accordingly. This is broadly called resource management, and includes capital and non-capital expenditure, recurrent and non-recurrent expenses and facility management. Staff wages will always take the largest chunk of the overall budget, approximately 60 per cent and sometimes more. Then money has to be allocated to facility upgrades, repairs and maintenance. There will be IT expenses for both staff and students. There will be a curriculum expense for everything from art supplies to musical instruments. Cleaning and landscaping form another expense. There will be sporting fields to mow and performance areas to clean, repair, maintain and upgrade, as well as courts, halls, theatres and gyms. There will be the usual bills to be paid for myriad items and utilities. All of this needs to be planned for in advance as much as feasibly possible and factored into the annual budget. Decisions need to be made around what is a must-have and what is a nice-to-have, what must be spent now and what can be postponed.

I liken resource management to the presence of an umpire or a referee: people won't generally notice it until something goes wrong. Classrooms need furniture, and they need it before the school year starts. Maintenance needs to be done, otherwise people get hurt. Teachers need laptops, otherwise they can't do their jobs. Timetable software needs to be purchased, otherwise we can't run the school. Viewed in isolation, these things all appear to be perfunctory decisions. In fact, a finite pool of money, time and people must to be allocated and balanced very carefully to make it through the year. If it's not done properly, the smooth functioning of a school can be derailed very quickly. You see, everyone wants a slice of the pie. Most staff don't care about a school budget, only wanting to hear about the allocations relevant to their role. I don't blame them. They didn't become educators to manage budgets or become pseudo project managers. That's not their job, it's yours.

When it comes to resource management, you've got to have a process and a plan. A process allows you to allocate time, funds and resources equitably and prudently. A plan allows you to have a timeline—short-term and long-term—to know when to allocate time, funds and resources equitably and prudently.

Process and plan

Part 1

When developing a resource management process and plan, you first need to highlight the core areas of school life and identify the sub-areas within each of these. The core areas are generally people, facilities, curriculum, equipment, co-curricular, operational and financial.

The following table is an example. It's not exhaustive, but it does cover most areas and sub-areas. Some will not have a monetary cost attached, but may instead have a human or time cost.

Table 1: Core school areas and sub-areas of school life

Area	Sub-area
People	Development & training Recruitment Appraisal Performance management
Facilities	Transport Maintenance Security Utilities—water Utilities—electricity Utilities—gas Air-conditioning Gym / fitness area Toilets & changerooms—staff & students Car parks—staff & parents Science lab Hospitality / kitchens Staff rooms Art / design Industrial design spaces Sport & HPE Capital works Lockers / locks Shade & seating Pathways, steps & handrails
Operational	Website Marketing Incursions Excursions Camps Transport—hire Timetable software LMS SMS Venue bookings Events Photocopying / paper

Area	Sub-area
Financial	Payroll Insurance Fees and debtors
Curriculum	Subscriptions Recurrent Non-recurrent Library Novels / texts
Equipment	IT Photocopiers Grounds equipment Hospitality equipment Design tech equipment Art / music equipment General classroom furniture
Co-curricular	Fields / courts / theatres / gyms Venue hire Bus hire Coach & tutor costs Sporting equipment Music equipment

The next table is one method to give your approach to resource management some structure. For the purposes of this exercise, I have selected only a few sub-areas. Once done in entirety, it would inform the annual budget with funds allocated to all areas of school life to be managed by specific individuals.

Table 2: Details of core areas and sub-areas of school life

Area	Sub-area	Explanation / description	Annual cost (000's)	Timeframe for purchase, upgrade or install	Supplier	Person	Notes
People	Development & training	First aid, fire safety & ASD (aspirating smoke detectors)		Spread across year	Independent Schools Queensland, First Aid Kits Australia	Principal	
	Recruitment	External recruitment company		On a needs basis	anzuk or Randstad	Principal	
Facilities	Transport	Bus operations, maintenance & bus hire		Quarterly	Local bus company & college mini-bus	Head of operations	Bus costs—internal & bus hire for events
	Maintenance	Window blinds, aircon, paint & locks		Ongoing	Bunnings, Mitre 10	Facilities manager	
	Security	CCTV, patrols & lighting		On a needs basis	Electrician	Facilities manager	
	Utilities—water	Regular expense		Quarterly	Urban Utilities	Finance manager	
Operational	Website	Creation & maintenance		Annual	Roberts Digital	Marketing officer	
	Marketing	Yearbook, prospectus & handbooks		Bi-annual	School Printers Co.	Marketing officer	

Area	Sub-area	Explanation / description	Annual cost (000's)	Timeframe for purchase, upgrade or install	Supplier	Person	Notes
Financial	Payroll	Including salary & superannuation Including daily relief costs & all leave entitlements		Fortnightly	TASS	Finance manager	
	Insurance	General liability, workers comp etc.		Annual	AON	Finance manager	
Curriculum	Subscriptions	Curriculum, digital texts, professional learning e.g. Mathletics		Annual	Various	Head of teaching & learning	
	Recurrent	Items that are used up within 12 months e.g. art supplies		Ongoing	Hart Sport, ART Supplies	Head of teaching & learning	
Equipment	IT	Staff & student laptops Data projectors Internet Servers Infrastructure costs		Annual	Brennan IT, MOQ Digital	Head of operations	Laptops on a 3-year lease
	Photocopiers	Secondary, primary, library, admin		Annual	Canon, Toshiba	Finance manager	
	Grounds equipment	Tools, mowers, hedgers etc.		Ongoing	Mitre 10	Facilities manager	
	Hospitality equipment	Coffee machine, cutlery, mixers etc.		Bi-annual	Hospitality Superstore	Head of hospitality	
Co-curricular	School musical	Upper primary & secondary students		T1 readiness & T3 performance	Art supplies, music instruments, hall venue hire	Head of arts	T1, 2 & 3 expense

Part 2

Remember that school budgets in Australia run for a calendar year, not a financial year. Preparation for a whole-school budget starts in September at the latest. Think of it as a Term 4 job that you complete in readiness for the year ahead.

1. Lock in your big-ticket expenses first: capital works, staffing, salaries.
2. Lock in your projected income: estimated enrolments, tuition fees, levies, government grants, philanthropic / fundraising.
3. Request wish-lists from staff who have extra responsibilities. Give them a format to add their estimated costs, quotes and research. Make them justify any major or out-of-the-ordinary expense.
4. Make decisions at senior leadership level about what is affordable, feasible, reasonable and in alignment with the strategic plan of the school.
5. The business manager and the principal prepare the budget and inform the board or head office. They then let staff know what they have available to spend. Some items are purchased at the end of the year to ensure delivery for the start of the new school year.

Part 3

A collection of other processes needs to be in place to ensure a school's smooth functioning. These include personal leave, professional learning, purchases and event organising. If your school already has these processes in place, then go to the next chapter.

Once a process is established and approved, there needs to be four-way communication at a minimum:

- Does the person responsible for daily relief know?
- Do the front office admin staff know?
- Does your line manager know?
- Do key personnel such as bus drivers, facility managers and coaches know?

If it is an event:

- Has it been communicated via the calendar, an email to parents, a post on social media, the newsletter or a conversation with any affected staff?
- Has the venue been booked, the bus hired, equipment rented, ground staff informed, lunch organised, first aid arranged, risk assessments done?
- Has it been organised four weeks in advance or has it been doomed to failure by being slapped together at the last moment? If it's the latter, congratulations! You now move from resource management to incident management and performance management.

Tips to make things easier

Be upfront and honest if you are responsible for making decisions around allocation. You'll need to follow a strategic plan and an annual operating plan. If you get pressured to upgrade the netball and volleyball courts when the arts are clearly slotted in first, remind people that plans have already been made and that there are priorities for a reason.

Review the budget regularly. This way you won't reach July with everything spent. Set your maintenance plan early in the year, and preferably at the end of the previous year. This should be part of the overall facility management strategy.

Make sure that staff who are submitting spending requests understand the difference between want and need. That second or third 3D printer may not be a priority for the tech department if the regular primary or secondary school printer is on its last legs.

If you have to make tough decisions around what to cut, always go to the non-core aspects of school life first: excursions and incursions, camps, external professional learning, daily relief, subscriptions, printing and photocopying.

If budgets are really tight then you'll need to look at staffing. Which classes can be combined? Which ancillary staff can be made redundant or simply not replaced if they resign?

Key takeaway

Resource management is complex. It's a constant process. It takes collaboration across all staffing areas. It's not the most exciting part of a leader's job, but it's one of the most important. With a little forward planning and transparency, you can also make it one of the most efficient.

11

Leading staff

Lesson #12 *The quickest way to lose the trust of your staff is to ask them to do something that you either can't or won't do yourself. Do the hard carry.*

It's not hard to find advice on people leadership. From my experience, much of it is nebulous and superficial. For instance, you've probably read about the need to lead with integrity and build a high-trust team. What does this actually mean, though, and how do we do it on a daily basis? Furthermore, has the person giving the advice acquired these insights from leading their own organisation or are they just some consultant who has the degrees and the slick marketing shtick?

Personally, I usually sit up and take notice from someone who's earned the battle scars by practicing what they preach. Here are 10 pieces of hard-earned wisdom from someone who has lived and breathed school leadership. You won't see most of these included in any Ted Talk or leadership seminar, but they work. Try them out if you want to build trust and integrity with the people you lead.

Foolproof strategies

Walk the halls

Whatever the leadership position you hold, your staff need to see you regularly. Don't lead via email, and don't be bound to your desk or your office. Firing off emails between other commitments might make you believe that you've connected with your colleagues or shared the latest decision with everyone. Sure, it might seem an efficient way to remind people of something that you feel is important before you go to your next meeting or leave for the day. But your staff need more from you than that. If it were as easy as shooting off a few emails then anyone could do it. You've got to get out.

You can achieve many different things by being out and about during the school day. Before and after school at pick-up and drop-off times, it allows parents to see you. During class time, it allows you to see teachers in action, without warning, to get a feel for how they are really going. You can also connect with students as they are learning. During lesson change-overs and break times, it allows you to help colleagues with playground duty, to pick up litter, to build a connection with kids. At the end of break, you can help move kids off to class on time.

You won't be able to do this every day, and you can't always pick your moment to get out. But your presence in the grounds, the hallways, the classrooms, the carparks and the sporting facilities is very important and greatly appreciated.

Do it yourself

Don't ask a staff member to do something that you yourself can't or won't do. You have to role-model what you expect to see from your staff. Don't worry, I don't mean installing a new veranda—if you're anything like me, your carpentry skills are poor and there are people far more experienced and qualified to do this job. I'm talking about being an example in the ways that you teach, address students, conduct yourself with parents, turn up every day. If teachers are expected to have student surveys done on them, then you get one done first. If you expect them to clip kids about uniform, then you show them how. And if you expect them to maintain excellent LMS hubs, then you need to do so as well if you teach a class or subject.

Don't kill with kindness

Are you aware of something that isn't appropriate? Do you have knowledge of poor performance or poor conduct? Then you need to do something. If you say nothing or communicate in a way that doesn't convey the seriousness of the situation, you are not doing anyone any favours. You are being false or disingenuous. Don't let your desire to be liked override your need to be honest. You don't have to be nasty or aggressive or condescending. You can be both kind and honest.

Standards

Standards indicate our expectations for the conduct and performance of staff and students. What you are willing to walk past becomes the standard you accept and the standard you set. If you are a leader and do not support the decisions of your leadership team or maintain the agreed standards, then hand in your badge and do not accept your extra time release or remuneration. You are an imposter. School leadership teams should come together at regular intervals to decide on expectations for everything from staff attire to student arrival times.

Appraisal and feedback

You've got to have a process in place to evaluate and provide feedback on teacher performance. It's a mandatory part of ongoing school accreditation, but it also ensures a healthy culture of improvement. As a school leader, you need to embrace formal and informal feedback. Formal feedback will take the form of appraisal, a clearly defined process that should be informed by at least three pieces of data. Informal feedback will be exchanged during the day-to-day mentoring relationship forged between teacher and school leader.

Develop your people

One of your core responsibilities as a leader is to develop the people around you. The people with whom you have the most contact are the ones whose collaboration you rely on to achieve collective goals. Building good relationships with your colleagues is important for both practical and ethical reasons. What's interesting is that if you do the ethical thing, the practical takes care of itself.

Levels of investment

Split your staff into three groups, and put your focus and energy towards the first two.

There is always a group of staff who largely want to be left alone. These people are capable, reliable and self-sufficient, experienced enough to know what they are doing and happy to get on with things as long as they have the time. They don't need their egos stroked, and they'll do an honest day's work for an honest day's pay. They like the place, they like the stability, they like the salary. They weather the ups and downs and keep turning up. They aren't particularly ambitious. Look after these people because they will look after you.

Then there are the staff who are keen to progress. They have an ambitious glint in their eye. They are the early adopters, the cheerleaders who are looking to advance their careers and take opportunities to do so. Identify who these ambitious ones are, as they will drive your initiatives. Just temper their drive a little so they don't burn everyone out in the pursuit of their personal gain. Look at ways to keep them engaged, fulfilled and remaining at your school. You can do this by giving them projects to lead. They'll get it done and come back looking for more.

Then there's the third group of staff: those who will disapprove no matter what you do. These people are negative by nature. They're predisposed to think that new ideas won't work. They complain often and like to draw others to the cause. You'll think that you can win them over by including them, consulting them, sometimes even agreeing with them, but it will be a short-term gain only. Don't waste your time, but don't let them become toxic either.

Clarity

The staff at your school need to know who to go to for a specific event or task or consequence. This involves more than the consultation of an organisational chart. It starts with everyone knowing what their role is, and communicating this regularly across the organisation. This will reduce confusion, ambiguity, frustration and inefficiencies.

Roadmap

The phrase 'strategic plan' is enough to put most teachers to sleep. That doesn't mean, however, that they don't want to know the school's goals or how these are expected to be achieved. The start of the year is a logical time to share this sort of information with staff. Not only that, but it allows people to have input into items that require implementation. Some might have suggestions and some might have questions.

Try to group your overarching goals into strategic themes. For instance, there's usually something that needs to be built, refurbished or repaired. There's usually a goal related to the curriculum, one related to the workforce and another related to students.

Announcing your goals

Here's how I might communicate my roadmap for the year to staff in preparation for a meeting.

Hi folks, welcome to the new school year. Hope you had a great holiday. It's another busy year ahead for us. We have a number of things that we want to achieve, and our big goals for the year are:

1. *Complete the installation of our industrial kitchen so we can deliver vocational hospitality courses and operate a daily tuckshop. Our facility manager is leading this project and it's due for completion in April.*
2. *We identified last year via NAPLAN data that our literacy levels are declining. We are in need of a whole-school literacy plan. Our head of teaching & learning will lead this project and we will implement it in Semester 2.*

3. *Our teacher appraisal framework needs an upgrade to ensure that we benchmark ourselves against the AITSL Standards and can collect a broader array of data to inform feedback. Our deputy has developed a draft which we'll share this week, will seek your feedback on and aim to roll out this term.*
4. *The number of expulsions and suspensions among our middle-school boys was excessive last year. We'd like to explore some measures to address this, so I'm calling for volunteers to be part of a working group led by the head of middle school.*

Time to plan

One of our most valuable commodities is time. We crave more of it in our personal lives and in our professional lives. Unfortunately, the administrative tasks assigned to teachers and school leaders affect our ability to set time aside for quality work, creativity, growth, collaboration and planning. Everyone will benefit if you can find ways to give staff some blocks of time to do these things.

How to find more time

- Don't fill staff days up with compliance training. You might be able to postpone it, break it up or move it online.
- Do parent-teacher interviews during school hours instead of in the evening.
- Extract some hours for project teams to complete work. If it is deemed so important, then give people the time and space to think.
- Evaluate your meeting schedule and decide what must be communicated in person and what can be covered via email.
- Think about who really needs to be at school events. Can some staff be released to do other work?

Acknowledgements

Most people don't need a big song and dance made about them to acknowledge a personal achievement or something they've done to make things happen. They don't generally put their hand up in the hope that it will get them noticed. They do things because they want to make a difference in the life of a student, a team, a group, a class, a colleague or the broader school community. A principal with a big staff won't know everything that's going on or be aware of every individual contribution. But an acknowledgement—whether public or via a small gift or personalised note—will be well received.

All power to you if you've got the capacity to keep track of everything and can regularly organise a note, a gift or a few words at a gathering. If you don't have that capacity, then lean on your admin staff to assist you. Often they know more about these things than you do. An acknowledgement will go a long way towards building a positive culture. It helps to bank goodwill that you can draw upon whenever needed. Acknowledgement makes people willing to go the extra mile, to volunteer the next time.

Key takeaway

Most often, it's the things that can't be measured that will bring success to your school. Building a culture of trust, integrity and high performance starts with you. Do the hard yards and show staff, students and parents what you're about.

12

Leading students

Lesson #13 *If you and your staff aren't united in your approach to leading students, you're wasting your time. Don't be that person who tries to be liked by the kids only to undermine your colleagues.*

Leading students is different to managing students. If you're managing them, you're employing strategies to mitigate poor behaviour and ensure compliance. It's not particularly inspiring; it's a way of making mass education possible. Leading is something bigger. Leading means getting your students to understand that they are being asked to act in their own best interests or for the greater good. We want them to do the right thing because they want to, not because they have to. Leaders cultivate that intrinsic motivation.

I'm not here to deliver awe-inspiring, wet-your-pants, jaw-dropping bombs of leadership inspiration. You know the kind: it sounds good, but a little testing reveals it to have very little practical application. Instead, I'd like to share a bunch of strategies that make perfect sense, are utterly practical and achievable, and can be applied almost immediately with a bit of intestinal fortitude and prior planning.

Foolproof strategies

Everyone needs to pull in the same direction

This one applies to staff. If your collective desire is to make sure all the kids get to class on time, or don't carry a mobile phone in their pocket, or remember to tuck their shirts in, or pick up their own rubbish and put it in the bin, then you all need to reinforce these expectations as soon as you see them being challenged in the playground or the classroom.

Kids need structure

Unless you subscribe to the free-range-chicken philosophy of learning, it is my strong belief that all children benefit from a very clear structure. This structure pertains to expectations around what to wear, how to conduct oneself in class and at events, and how to move around a school. Structure is about providing a foundation upon which everything else is based. It is in fact the bedrock of creativity and innovation. Structure ensures that everyone has an opportunity to excel, rather than allowing the noisy minority to dominate. Kids also need certainty, and structure provides this.

Fairness

The law of the jungle is alive and well in schools, particularly in the playground. One of the rules of this law pertains to perceptions of fairness. Nothing will damage your integrity with kids more than the belief they have been unfairly treated, that you're negatively biased against them, or that you continue to hold a grudge for any past misdemeanours. You do any of these things, and you've lost them. Once this happens, it's very hard to get them back. When you want to facilitate a student leadership workshop, they won't listen. When you're up at assembly talking about values or expectations, they won't listen.

Fairness in this case applies to a variety of things. It includes the consequences dished out to different kids for the same offence. It includes rewards and acknowledgements for similar actions and performances. It includes things like not always picking the same student or group to pick up litter, stack chairs after an assembly or tidy up the classroom after an event.

Sometimes there are extenuating circumstances when differing consequences or rewards must be applied, and these can't always be spelled out to students. It's easy to say that this is none of their business and that things get done at your discretion. But that won't wash, particularly with older kids. In this situation, I suggest you at the very least explain to the students concerned why a decision was made. The very fact that you are giving them the time for a rationale will go a long way, and if you have already banked a degree of trust with them that will help immensely.

The rule of 3

Here's a trick that's quite versatile and a good rule of thumb for effective communication. Want to get a message across? Repeat it 3 times, use 3 methods and stick to 3 points only.

Don't expect kids to remember everything you tell them straight away. One third will retain the information the first time they hear it, another third will understand when you repeat it, and the remaining students will jump on board the last time around. Sure, there might be a few outliers. But if the vast majority know what is going on, the remaining clueless souls will get swept along with the masses.

The rule of 3 can also be applied to the number of things that you want students to remember:

1. Get to class on time
2. Charge your laptops overnight
3. No hat, no play

In a more general sense, it can be applied to the number of communication methods you use:

1. Assembly
2. Email
3. Facebook

Map out the school year

Get a large whiteboard for your office and map out your entire school year from January to December. This gives you a constant visual of all four terms. Your whiteboard should contain major dates such as public holidays, student-free days, parent-teacher interviews, camps, information events, awards ceremonies and sporting carnivals.

This allows you to plan effectively. It also allows student captains and key staff to have the same overview whenever they come into your office. Schools are extremely busy places, and staff and students often have multiple commitments. Your year-level coordinators or heads of house will also be teaching and managing assessment, marking and reporting. These same teachers might coach a team or supervise debating. They might need to attend a camp. They might be organising science week or book week or the Year 12 valedictory dinner. The same applies to your students: they have their own assessment schedules, plus training and games, or participating in the musical, or attending a camp. Your ability to support your students—and the staff who support those students—will ensure balance and sanity.

The 4-weeks-ahead rule

As a school leader, you need to stay four weeks ahead. While the rest of the school is enjoying the events of the current week, you'll already be planning everything that is to occur within the next month. Four weeks is my rough schedule to live by when school events really need to start being organised. Plenty of things are booked 12 months in advance: camps, venues, major events. These are basically set-and-forget... until the 4-weeks-ahead rule kicks in. Use your whiteboard to provide a visual map of things to come.

Events

View events as an opportunity to develop student leadership. Every event is a project-management goldmine. There is stuff to organise, book and plan. There are a range of communication pieces. There are the human resources elements. Not every event has to be solely planned by you or other staff members.

Students can do the following:

- Speak at assembly
- Prepare the floor plan
- Act as ushers
- Make posters
- Coach the younger grades
- Lead the long-jump or discus-throwing events
- Collect money
- Cook sausages
- Man the fete stall
- Run lunchtime activities
- Help with setting up and packing up
- Run the tech system
- Help in the carpark pick-up zone

Even if they shadow you initially, these are teachable moments.

The other thing that events do is teach students about appropriate conduct for an occasion, and the symbolism of different occasions. Schools are choc-full of these opportunities, and your job as a school leader is to educate students about the purpose and history of events. These may include:

- Remembrance Day ceremony
- ANZAC Day ceremony
- Athletics, swimming and cross-country carnivals
- Awards nights
- Year 7 orientation day
- Book week parade
- Grade 6 graduation
- Year 12 valedictory
- Year 11 semi-formal and Year 12 formal
- Scholars assembly
- Prep open night

As a school leader, you're not just showing up. You're passing on knowledge about the reasoning behind what everyone is doing, and you're teaching kids how to lead, facilitate, communicate, deal with setbacks, manage time and manage people.

Be seen and be heard

As a school leader you need to build your brand. To state the obvious, you can't lead from behind your desk. You need to be on your feet walking the grounds, visiting classrooms, helping with duties and being highly visible. This achieves a few things. You connect with kids and build a relationship with them. You have a calming presence. You can mitigate little incidents before they become big incidents. You build credibility and collegiality with colleagues.

You need to find a suitable voice for each occasion. You should have a classroom voice, an assembly voice, a staff meeting voice, a playground voice and a voice that makes the kids walk a bit quicker. You need to be comfortable with speaking at assemblies, to large groups of parents and at staff meetings. On top of that, you need to develop a presence. Consider the way you carry yourself, the way you dress, the way you speak. Don't do these things with arrogance or ego or overconfidence. Develop an appropriate level of authority, of gravitas dipped in kindness and humility. Think about your message and how you deliver it. If you talk in a monotone voice, drone on for too long or waffle too much, whatever message you are trying to convey will get lost. Keep it on point, keep it purposeful, use emphasis and pause at key points, make eye contact, and do not read word-for-word from a script unless it is a formal occasion. As Dylan Thomas put it, *Do not go gentle into that good night.* Find your inner steel.

Pick your battles

Remember my point about the standard you accept being the standard you walk past? This one's about deciding what you are prepared to die on a hill for. You need to pick your battles, especially when you find yourself at a school where there are so many issues that you don't know where to begin. One of my schools had a huge problem with uniform. As a staff collective, we identified the Big 5 items that mattered most to us. We started enforcing our expectations: shirt tucked in, wear a belt, no nose rings, black leather shoes, correct school bag. We didn't waste time or energy on anything else. We correctly figured that if we got those things right, other things would soon follow.

Humour and vulnerability

You gotta know when to hold 'em, know when to fold 'em—so goes the line from the oft-heard 'The Gambler' by the late Kenny Rogers. When leading students, you have to know when to be a disciplinarian and when to show a gentler side. Using humour and showing vulnerabilities helps to build a relationship with students. You can't lead with the authoritarian mask on for too long. Students respond well to school leaders whom they respect and can also have a joke with. This rapport can only be developed if the authoritarian mask is dropped and the real human emerges.

Develop student leadership from within

If we want to have strong leaders in Year 12, we need to have a student leadership program that starts in upper primary. In the corporate world, the CEO, GM and board chair commence their roles with training, qualifications and experience. So why would we expect anything different of a teenager? In so many schools, we have a bunch of kids in Year 11 being asked to consider a leadership role in Year 12 without much training or exposure. When they do start in these roles, they don't have the skills, insights or confidence to do well in the role. We expect them to get up at assembly in front of hundreds of people and speak fluently and strongly, when most of the adults in the room couldn't do it themselves.

Key takeaway

Leading students is different to managing students. While a level of authority is required, it doesn't mean that you need to be authoritarian in your approach. Effective leaders understand the value of nuance and good humour. A strong rapport between students and leadership goes a long way towards ensuring proactive compliance with rules and expectations. Remember that what may seem obvious to the adults in the room may have to be spelled out to the kids. Keep your patience, and give your students the opportunity to build their skills and confidence with real responsibilities.

13

Leading parents

Lesson #14 *Facilities are nice, but they are less important than the level of genuine care that teachers and leaders have for a child.*

Parents are key stakeholders in the life of a school. Your relationship with them is a partnership and one that needs to be worked on. The nuances of this partnership may be affected by the type of school you run and the choices that parents make in sending their children there. In the case of fee-paying schools, the parent is a customer who pays for a service that they don't directly consume but indirectly benefit from through their children. In the case of public schooling, some parents may simply be fulfilling their legal obligation to send their children to school until the age of 16 by making a choice within their local catchment.

As a school leader, you should approach the educational life of a child as a three-way partnership: school-child-home. The following suggestions should assist you in making this partnership as effective as possible.

Foolproof strategies

The moment of enquiry

The goal of the school leader is to ensure that every part of the school journey for a parent is positive, or at least not disappointing. This begins before their child has even joined your school.

The journey starts with an initial enquiry from a parent. This could be before the commencement of Prep or it could be in preparation for their child changing schools at another year level. The initial enquiry is most likely to occur via the website. The parent will be looking to see what the school offers and trying to get a feel for the climate, values and culture of the place. The next step is a phone call, an email or an online enquiry form. Make this process as painless as possible, and regularly review your website to ensure that it's not only up-to-date but accurately represents how you want your school to be perceived.

Value for money

Regardless of whether we are talking public or private, parents want and deserve value for money. If their kids are attending a public school, they aren't paying much in tuition fees. But the majority are paying taxes and often various levies. If they are paying tuition fees at an independent school, there is an added expectation of value for money. For $20,000 per year, parents want their child to at least get a B average, to learn an instrument and a language, to establish a rich network of friends and acquaintances to participate in a sport of choice and to be morally and socially competent by the end of Year 12.

The independent school parent is also paying for something called 'social capital'. The facilities are a bit nicer, the learning support is a bit more extensive, there are broader co-curricular choices. Really, however, these parents are choosing a school where their child can acquire core values that align with their own world view, where they can mix with other kids who later in life might prove useful contacts for work and opportunities.

Communication channels

Like the rest of us, parents are time-poor. They're juggling work, family, businesses, health and extended family. There is a fine line between over-communication and under-communication, and this line is different for everybody. Before the digital world, the hardcopy newsletter was the main source of regular whole-school communication. No apps, email, website, texting or social media—yet we all seemed to know what was going on. People today consume their news in different ways, and you have to be thoughtful about the methods you use to communicate with them.

Some parents read everything and enjoy regular updates. Others get overwhelmed with constant communication and rarely if ever engage with whatever school business comes across their newsfeed. My recommendation is that it is better to over-communicate. Parents can always curate what they want to read and when.

My second suggestion is to use different channels as effectively as you can. Try to direct parents towards your LMS and website. Provide a link if you're sending out sensitive or important information of the type found in newsletters, academic reports and strategic plans.

My final recommendation is to have a matrix to manage the type, amount and channel of school communications. For instance: if the behaviour of a child in Year 9 is such that it could easily provoke an email home from every teacher every day, then it's best that a single communication to their parents should come from the year level co-ordinator or head of house.

No surprises

Things shouldn't get to the point where parents hear about the poor conduct of their child for the first time at a termination-of-enrolment meeting or a one-week suspension meeting. It is of course possible that the kid had a complete brain snap and acted out of character, in which case this will likely be the first conversation of its kind. Similarly, things shouldn't get to the point where the academic failure of a child only becomes apparent to their parents upon receipt of a report card.

Be seen

As a school leader, you need to be familiar to parents. Being out and about is a great way to build your identity, your profile, your brand. Not only should you be seen, but you should have conversations that foster relationships and understanding. Give parents some reassurance that you're an engaged leader who is aware of the pulse of the school, someone in whose hands they should want to place their child.

You can be seen on a variety of occasions:

- Pick-up and drop-off times—carpark, pathways, front gate, playgrounds
- School events—fetes, info nights, parent nights, parent-teacher interviews, book fair
- Assemblies that parents are invited to—they get to hear you speak

Partnerships

There are two types of parent partnership. The first type you need to cultivate with all parents, and the second type you need to cultivate with key parents or parent groups such as the P&F. 'Key parents' doesn't mean that some parents are more important than others. It means that some have certain characteristics, skills and connections that are beneficial to the school and your ability to implement initiatives or changes.

Workshops

Schools don't simply provide a formal education for children. They are also venues for parents to receive some education themselves. If you view parents as partners, then you'll see that upskilling them is an important part of school life. I recommend running workshops. These might be solely for Mum and Dad or they might be for the entire family. See them as an opportunity to add value. Equipping parents with key competencies and building their confidence will have a positive impact on their children. Furthermore, workshops provide an avenue for parents to connect with each other.

Not all parents will attend, and those who don't are often the ones who would most benefit! Nevertheless, it is important to persevere. Workshops can be delivered by the counsellor, the academic leads, the principal or an external presenter.

Topics covered might include:

- Cybersafety
- Supporting teenage boys / girls
- Prep orientation
- Adolescent mental health
- Supporting the academic life of your child
- A focus on key points of the school journey (the middle and senior years)
- Consent education
- Bullying and friendship
- Parenting

Access

I don't mean access via the front gate. I mean access to teachers and to information. The school needs to make engagement easy for parents by removing potential barriers. Some parents have a negative perception of school left over from their own childhood. Some are intimidated by the institution or the staff. Some have poor IT skills. If they are immigrants or refugees, they may lack the language skills, the know-how and the confidence to enquire and engage.

Some schools are not particularly warm or welcoming, and actively try to keep parents at arm's length. Some have a mentality of 'we teach kids and parents can please themselves'. Some have IT platforms that require a degree in computer science to download the latest academic report card. Don't let this be your school!

Unpack and reduce 'eduspeak'

Acronyms, terminology and educational catchphrases are used all across the education industry. Most of these are very familiar to teachers, but provoke complete bewilderment in parents.

If native-born English-speaking parents find the eduspeak dialect difficult to comprehend, what hope do newly-arrived immigrants have?

Let's have a look at the following examples (and many of these are just for Queensland). There are plenty more that could be listed, but I'd run out of paper!

- QCAA – Queensland Curriculum and Assessment Authority
- ATAR – Australian Tertiary Admission Rank
- QCE – Queensland Certificate of Education
- ISQ – Independent Schools Queensland
- QCT – Queensland College of Teachers
- NSSAB – Non-State Schools Accreditation Board
- NCCD – Nationally Consistent Collection of Data
- NAPLAN – National Assessment Program – Literacy and Numeracy
- RTO – Registered training organisation
- VET – Vocational Education and Training
- SETP – Student Education and Training Plan
- WWCC – Working with Children Check
- SEO – Senior Education Officer
- SSO – School Support Officer
- RPL – Recognition of prior learning
- MCEECDYA – Ministerial Council of Education, Early Childhood Development and Youth Affairs
- LOTE – Language other than English
- EAL – English as an additional language
- ASD – Autism Spectrum Disorder

Here is a list of terminology that educators often hear and talk about among ourselves, yet many parents would have little idea of:

- Pedagogy
- Differentiation
- General and Applied subjects
- Streaming
- Higher-order thinking
- Bloom's taxonomy
- Maslow's hierarchy
- Inquiry learning
- Learning to learn
- 21st-century learning
- Project-based learning
- Learning by design
- Visible learning
- Self-directed learning
- Explicit teaching

Honestly, it's an absolute minefield! If you can take the time to really explain some of this to parents when you do communicate with them, they will be eternally grateful.

Eduspeak: how not to communicate

Now have a read of this little example below. It's a letter to a parent. If they can interpret it then you might want to employ them, as they have a better grasp of educational jargon than most teachers.

Dear Mrs Smith

Your child Gary has expressed a desire to pursue an ATAR via two potential pathways including General subjects and a VET option with our preferred RTO. Whilst our pedagogy at school has tended to focus more on self-directed learning, we feel that it's in Gary's best interests to pursue these pathways as it will give him the best chance to attain his QCE. He may even be eligible for RPL which we can explore at our upcoming SETP meeting.

Kind regards

Mr D Vader

Deputy

Key takeaway

Understand that parents have certain expectations and desires from their child's school. These may relate to academics, sport, the arts, networking or values. As a leader, you need to decide what your school stands for. What's its niche? How does it add value? If a parent had a choice, why would they decide to send their child to your school and not a neighbouring one? If you were to ask them what was unique about your school that separated it from the rest, what would they say?

14

The Wisdom story: A case study

Lesson #15 When building or rebuilding a school, start with people first and structures second. Systems, platforms and frameworks should come last. If you don't know what you want the school to stand for, you can't put things in place to help you get there.

I write this case study as the current principal of Wisdom College. I am incredibly proud of the school community for what we have collectively achieved, not just in my time here but since the inception of the College in 2012, and for the foresight that existed even well before then. I have included this chapter to illustrate my lived experience of school leadership. No names have been included apart from that of a member of the senior leadership team. It is my hope that my experiences may help other school leaders and their communities.

Background

Wisdom College is a multicultural, non-denominational yet Islamic-inspired P-12 school founded by the local Turkish Muslim community on the south side of Brisbane. There are over 40 different cultural and ethnic groups among the student population, but Islam is the dominant faith. This is reflected in a number of ways: a prayer room, an imam on staff, the observance of significant events such as Ramadan and Eid, the hosting of iftar dinners, the onsite delivery of the Jummah Friday prayer and the teaching of Arabic. The College's underlying philosophy—to promote understanding, peace, co-existence and service to others—is based on the values of Hizmet, a faith-based civil society movement founded by Turkish scholar Fethullah Gülen.

In 2021, I began as Wisdom's first non-Muslim principal. In the 10 years prior to my arrival, there had been four principals. It is safe to say that the board, the staff and those previous principals had all been well-meaning, with a genuine desire to create a quality educational experience. Most people at the College were indeed warm and welcoming. I noticed quickly, however, that the school suffered from a number of inconsistencies, gaps and weaknesses. I saw these as opportunities. Here was a chance to create a truly multicultural school where all faiths were embraced and celebrated, and where we could be agile enough to be innovative and entrepreneurial in our approach to schooling.

The parents were kind and accepting of me, at least to my face. I knew that there were some doubters, but any new principal encounters those. For the first time in my career, though, I wanted to see more of the invisible doubters. Parents were not highly involved, and most information events were attended primarily by staff. Despite already having seen off four principals, these staff were receptive to change and in fact embraced it. I think they were at a point where they were willing to buy in on the condition that I stuck around, had a reasonably decent plan for the College and seemed to know what I was doing.

Although lacking fundamental learning habits, the students were in the main friendly, happy and compliant. They were, however, very raw. Many, especially in the secondary grades, had minimal ability to focus for any length of time, to engage in productive learning, to wear a uniform, to complete homework (or any work for that matter!), or to come to class with all the requisite learning utensils. Many of them looked at me initially as just another person passing through, and quite a few tested me to see if I would stick around. But that was just part of the fun in those early days. The board also recognised that they needed to improve their understanding of school governance practices; they just didn't know how. To their credit, they had the courage to appoint me in the first place. I think they figured that we were all in this together, so they might as well get behind me.

I must stress that there was a core of very committed staff who worked with me every step of the way to implement change. We were a team in every sense. They were and remain exceptional educators, passionate and extremely hardworking. All of them were receptive to change, and they supported each other and backed me at all times. Alongside their formal roles they did so much for the benefit of the College and the wider community. I learnt so much from them and remain in awe of them. I must also acknowledge the wonderful support of Mrs Ayse Dogan, who was the acting principal before my arrival and became the head of teaching and learning. Thank you, my friends.

Identifying what needed to change

Every school, regardless of age or wealth, has challenges unique to its context and history. The gaps, inconsistencies and weaknesses at Wisdom College could be grouped into the following categories:

Governance

There was a lack of knowledge around what school governance was and how it should be applied.

Vision, mission and philosophy

The College was to all intents and purposes Islamic. It had an Islamic board, was supported by the local Muslim community and had a Muslim founder. The majority of its students were Muslim. However, it called itself multicultural and non-denominational. Our school identity was therefore uncertain and ambiguous.

Facilities and resource management

There was no clear budget framework, no formal approach to the repair and maintenance of facilities, and minimal procedures governing risk and WHS.

Strategy and annual operational plan

Most of the planning focused on the curriculum. There was no tangible strategy beyond 12 months, and no obvious plan around staff development.

Staff

A staff appraisal process existed, but it lacked rigour and depth. Minimal professional learning plans were in place.

Curriculum

We had no teaching and learning framework, minimal curriculum maps and no clear team to oversee and drive curriculum processes for P-12. Some pastoral care existed, but it was segmented and not built into the timetable.

Students

Our students suffered from a lack of habits, expectations and structures, particularly in secondary.

Making the change happen

There was a lot of work to do, and it needed to be done in a specific order (albeit with plenty of overlap at times). Underpinning everything was my desire to build trust, competence, integrity and relationships.

Define your 'who'

We were trying to appeal to everyone without standing for anything, and we needed to establish who we were. The school was clearly Islamic. By denying this we were being disingenuous to non-Muslim enrolments and not fully embracing our heritage. We followed the Islam-inspired humanism of the Hizmet movement, but were almost reluctant to talk about it. There was a lack of knowledge about what Hizmet stood for and a failure to articulate it anywhere. A minority of staff were called Hizmet staff because they had attended a Hizmet school or grew up in a family that practiced Hizmet teachings.

Here we had a school that was clearly Islamic, taught Arabic, delivered values lessons in the Islamic tradition, had an imam on staff and celebrated all the key Islamic events, yet called itself non-denominational. We were supposed to be a Hizmet school, yet few knew what this meant. Nor was there a clear program of service learning—a core value of Hizmet.

So we educated our staff about Hizmet. We included the word and an explanation of the movement, its founder, its history and its core values in all our publications, at parent gatherings and on social media. We established a service-learning program.

We decided to call ourselves *Islamic-inspired*. When non-Muslim parents enquired about a potential enrolment they would be left with no confusion, and when Muslim parents wanted to do the same, they too had a clear understanding of what to expect.

Clarify the organisational structure

We redesigned the entire organisation. When I arrived, too many roles lacked clear purpose and reporting lines. We needed to create roles to address important things that weren't getting done across the various spheres of school life including curricular, co-curricular and operations. There were no position descriptions for most roles, so we had people who didn't know what was expected of them and therefore no-one else who knew either. Some roles were made obsolete, and new roles were created. We redrew the organisational chart so that there were very clear lines of reporting. Due to the redesign, everyone had to re-apply for their existing roles alongside anyone else who was interested. I bought in an experienced external educator to assist me with the recruitment process. We appointed and commenced.

Move some people off the bus

People typically leave an organisation in one of three ways:

- They find a wonderful opportunity elsewhere and go on to fulfil a career aspiration
- They see that things are changing, so they leave voluntarily—perhaps their power base is eroding, things don't suit their world view or they are no longer happy
- They are strongly encouraged to leave or facilitated to depart by leadership because they are underperforming, incompetent or toxic

All three of these things happened at Wisdom within my first 12 months.

Attract and retain staff

To make Wisdom an appealing place to work, I knew that I needed to do a few things:

- Align teacher salaries with standards set by the major employer of teachers in the state
- Find time for staff to plan, collaborate and bond without the excessive burden of what I call administrivia
- Provide professional learning opportunities and pathways that included mentoring, coaching and leadership training
- Build opportunities for career progression
- Grow everyone's trust in the principal, in the organisation and in each other

This last one is still a work in progress, which is not surprising because it's the only 'soft' skill on the list. There is, of course, nothing soft about it. A culture of trust is one of the hardest goals to achieve, but I intend to get there.

How do I plan on doing this? Instead of the KISS principle (Keep It Simple, Stupid), I follow the KIT principle (Kindness, Inclusion, Transparency). Most other things take care of themselves if I do these three things consistently.

To carve out time for planning, collaborating and bonding we did the following:

- Instead of parent-teacher interviews being conducted after school over a period of several days, we created a student-free day and wrapped them up by 4pm.
- We created small teams to focus on projects that had an end goal. To create a teaching and learning framework, we pulled together a team of four staff, hired a hotel meeting room up the road and released the team for the day to work on the project while we covered their classes.
- At the end of semester, we gathered all students together in the secondary school and ran some mini sporting carnivals and gala days. Kids would get to play sport all day while the teachers went off to work on the curriculum. Sometimes I managed to gather a few university students majoring in health and physical education to act as coaches, and once I even brought in my own older boys. The head of secondary and head of primary do similar activities to this day for the same purpose.
- We built in additional student-free days so that we had a total of 12 days spread across the school year, 5 of which were in the middle of the year to provide valuable time for staff to finish Semester 1 work and prepare for Semester 2.

I couldn't compete with most other independent schools on salary. We didn't have wonderful facilities with beautiful gyms, a swimming pool, industrial kitchens or workshops. We weren't even part of any sporting competition, and there was no choir or band. We didn't have well-hewn and clearly defined middle-leadership roles such as head of department or head of house. I needed to find a few things that could separate Wisdom from its competitors. The two that I settled on were time and innovation. Time for staff to plan, to complete professional learning, to mark, moderate and report, and to collaborate on projects. Innovation around how we could adjust the education model to suit our kids, rather than shoehorning the kids into the education model.

After 12 months had passed and enrolments had increased, the College started to evolve into a more sophisticated outfit. We established some additional middle leadership roles. This enabled me to hire experienced educators, and that's when things really started to snowball.

Get a strategy

We needed a roadmap. The operational plan in place was yearly and largely focused on the curriculum. Nothing wrong with that, but we needed something that transcended the single school year. This strategy needed to cover the core parts of school life: staff, community, parents, governance, finances, learning, students and facilities. We also needed awareness, buy-in and input from key stakeholders: parents, staff, students and the wider community. I wanted to know how Wisdom College could serve people's dreams, ambitions and needs.

I facilitated workshops for staff, the board and key community members, as well as focus groups for parents and senior students. Knowing that some staff and parents would not end up making these commitments, I also conducted anonymous surveys. I actively sought feedback from parents at morning teas for mothers, at drop-off and pick-up times in the carpark, at awards ceremonies and special assemblies. We did a demographic analysis of our parents and their professions, and of the suburbs we drew our students from. I did an analysis of our competitors across the Catholic, independent and government sectors.

Through all of this, I distilled priorities down to six areas: learning, people, students, community, facilities, and governance and sustainability. Each priority area had five goals, and each goal had five action items. Each action item had a due date and a name attached to it. This was operationalised into an annual document and reviewed each term by the senior leadership team. We used a traffic-light system to indicate progress against each goal. This formed the structure upon which I based my monthly board reports, my yearbook article and my annual general meeting report. The process established alignment between board-level and ground-level actionable items, and ensured the visibility of our strategic innovation. Everyone could see where we were going, how we were going to get there, our progress to date, and who was responsible for each piece.

I then established with the board the KPIs that we would use to measure progress: staff and parent satisfaction survey data, staff turnover, enrolment figures, facility upgrades, debt collection, wages as a percentage of expenses and delivery on projects, to name but a few.

Improve governance

When I first arrived at Wisdom College, I met a group of hardworking, community-connected board members who weren't driven by ego or agenda. Some were even reluctant to serve but did so out of a sense of duty. By the board's own admission, they lacked knowledge of what a well-functioning independent school looked like. What they did have, though, was an open mind, a desire to learn and a drive to improve. They were a close-knit group with no apparent factions or insurmountably differing opinions. They allowed me to run the school without any significant interference, which I know is not always the case. They were there to support and counsel me. Their advice was particularly useful around community and religious matters, and allowed me to approach issues in a culturally sensitive way.

Despite all this great work, however, the board was not particularly visible to staff and parents. I wanted to lift their profile, to get them more involved, to bridge the gap.

So what did we do?

I brought in an old friend, an expert in school finances and governance, to lead some training for the board and the senior leadership team.

I brought the board together outside of their usual meeting time to help us establish a vision and a strategy for the College. I wanted them to lift their heads above the weeds of a typical agenda to do some blue-sky thinking. I wanted to see their visions—collective and individual—and I wanted them to see mine. I also wanted them to know me better, for us to gel as a team. I knew that we could do this by spending time together, sharing a meal and a conversation.

We started to put in place sound governance principals. These were simple yet important things like a conflict-of-interest register, a risk register, action items, a list of decisions made, a policy review calendar and monthly reports from the board members, the chair and me.

I kept the board regularly informed. I didn't bother them with the mundane, but I did let them know about significant occurrences.

I invited them to all key school events. Sometimes they made it, and this gave them an opportunity to meet staff, build their profile and better understand their community.

Heal old wounds

In order to move forward, some relationships needed mending. Some wounds were important to heal, while others required a clean incision.

A lack of prior exposure to any relationship breakdowns across the College community granted me some degree of impartiality. This was both good and bad: for instance, I had no emotional baggage or perceived alignment with any group, person or segment. However, I also didn't know much about the past, so it was important that I reserve judgement. The history of any organisation is not easily forgotten, and I felt I needed to be careful in my observations to better understand the history of the College and use that understanding to inform any future decision-making.

There was no point in overthinking things. I was going to get busy, one way or another. Was I going to ignore the problems of the past, old grievances or supposed mistakes, and allow them to fester? Or was I going to start healing? I chose healing.

The effort to rebuild was a double-edged sword. Some people who were not happy with my appointment soon left the College. Others who had previously felt aggrieved came back. They re-enrolled their children and re-engaged as parents.

Our sister Hizmet schools in other parts of Australia and the world reconnected with us. They visited us, we visited them, we presented at conferences together, we started sharing resources and ideas.

We started to grow up as a school community. No longer could anyone say that decisions were made in the best interests of a particularly powerful faction of the College—real or perceived. All efforts now went towards the best interests of the students. The familial bonds on which the school was originally founded had been broken, a necessary step for the health of the community and the long-term sustainability of the school.

Get good people

With the organisational structure redesigned and new roles implemented, we had an opportunity to get a range of new people into the school. That's not to say there weren't good people already; there were plenty. But we did need particular skillsets. Often the successful applicants were not the most experienced, but they were the right fit with the necessary temperament and character traits. I hired for attitude before aptitude. Content can be taught, but kindness, decency and integrity cannot. I didn't always get it right, and I initially wasn't swamped with options, but I stuck to my plan.

Sometimes these people were already in the organisation and simply needed to be given confidence and the chance to try out for a role that would suit them better or reinvigorate them.

We sought not only good teachers but also good teacher aides, middle leaders, senior leaders and admin; people who were kind-hearted, collaborative and humble, with no dysfunctional ego. To borrow from James Kerr's wonderful book *Legacy*, the story behind the success of the New Zealand All Blacks, we had a no-idiot policy.

Wisdom College needed people from well-run schools; people who understood the ingredients of quality teaching and extracurricular activities. These staff would put processes in place for sporting carnivals, student leadership, house activities, professional development, budgets, staff meetings, timetabling, and the creation of yearbooks and marketing collateral.

Once we reached the point where people with the desired skills and experience made up more than 50 per cent of our staff, everything became so much easier. Student behaviour improved significantly. Processes and procedures were streamlined and embedded. Staff had certainty, consistency and expectations. Communication increased, and a culture of mentoring and coaching started to emerge.

Build existing people

There was now a need to build capacity, confidence and skills—particularly among the senior leaders. We implemented a mentoring and coaching approach, and I sourced external professional learning relevant to each role and growth area. We met regularly as individuals and as a team, spending time together offsite to build understanding and do some deeper work. I also organised a group visit to an established well-functioning school so they could see for themselves what success looked like.

Grow trust

As Wisdom's fifth principal in 10 years and its first non-Muslim principal, I knew I had to build trust as quickly as possible. This would be vital for us to successfully implement the changes that the College needed. I also had some evidence to suggest that a small minority of people across the College community were hoping for me to fail. They were passive aggressive towards me, and some actively undermined me. I think this happens in many organisations when the new guy or gal steps in and the power base for some people shifts. It had certainly happened to me at some of my previous schools, so it didn't surprise me when I felt it again.

I had a complex little environment to navigate. My first task was to pin up a list of things that a principal should do to build trust, from the research that my old mate Dr Paul Browning OAM did for his PhD. I used this list as my guide.

Throughout the term preceding my official commencement, I got out to the school as much as I could to meet everyone. I introduced myself to every member of staff individually and visited every classroom to say hello. These interactions allowed the school community to get familiar with me while I was building my understanding of the organisation.

As soon as I started, I facilitated three separate workshops for staff, students and parents. At the workshops, I asked two questions: where have we come from and where do we want to go? These occasions served a few purposes. They brought people together to work, laugh and chat over a cup of tea. They gave individuals an opportunity to contribute to something bigger than themselves. They showed my KIT principle of kindness, inclusion and transparency in action. They informed my strategic planning that was bubbling along in the background.

After the workshops, I sent summaries of the key points and themes to those involved. I told them that their responses would affect the future of the College, and that their contributions mattered.

I also taught a class. For the first time in my career, I was teaching English—in fact Senior English—and I loved it. I made this choice for a few reasons. The first reason was that all the other teachers were either at full load or had other subject areas. The second reason was that I wanted to get in the classroom to experience what that environment was like for my teaching staff and build a level of credibility with them. The third reason was that I wanted to establish a rapport with the students, to deeply understand their backgrounds and their barriers to learning.

When I started, there were separate timetables and house systems for primary and secondary. For a small school, we had nine houses in total! This created two separate groups of staff who couldn't be shared across Prep to Year 12, and made the secondary school appear to be tacked on as an afterthought to the original primary school. It also meant that we couldn't have whole-school sporting carnivals where students competed for their house. This built an invisible wall with little sharing and collaboration. So I created four houses from Prep to Year 12, and established a whole-school timetable with the same start and finish times, as well as break times. Now staff could move more easily across year levels, and the houses could be used as organising mechanisms as well as building school spirit.

Following the workshops, surveys, focus groups and data-gathering, I completed a number of projects upon the close of my first term (Term 4 of 2021). We now had a strategic plan, a new website, an updated organisational chart, new roles and people appointed to those roles. I pushed these projects out at the end of the year with the intention of revisiting them in early 2022 to make sure I had a very clear platform for change and improvement.

I had a feeling that one way that I could build trust and get some early wins was for people to actually see change. If I could highlight and action things that would make an immediate improvement, I knew I'd have an opening to enact other improvement measures without resistance. At Wisdom, this change came in the form of seating, shade and pathways—there was an acute need for all three.

Bring people together

People within a school community come together for food, sport, the arts, awards and assemblies. My time at previous schools taught me that the intended purpose of an event is sometimes less important than the social capital built when people come together.

I quickly realised that most parents at Wisdom would not attend something called Information Night, even if it covered senior schooling or career pathways. Some simply didn't see these events as important. Some were reluctant to engage with school because they had not had a good experience themselves as children, while others spoke English as a second language and feared that they wouldn't be able to grasp what was being shared. Many were simply too overwhelmed with family and work commitments.

In my previous time as a sports master, I had discovered that sporting carnivals were a great way to get staff to develop a team bond that they would carry for the rest of the school year. Picture it: you might be one of eight marshals at a swimming carnival, or one of four judges collating points and handing out ribbons. When you work with someone all day at the javelin, long jump or discus, you get to know them on a deeper level. Over that one day, you can develop a connection that would normally take a whole year to grow. Within my first 12 months at Wisdom, we had implemented a swimming carnival, a cross-country carnival and an athletics carnival. We already had an awards night, an end-of-year musical night, a fete and an iftar dinner. I leveraged all of these to my advantage and tweaked them to ensure that staff from different sections of the school were working together as much as possible.

Implement systems and platforms

Over are the days of the deputy principal creating and managing a timetable and daily relief on a whiteboard. Over are the days of the teacher manually marking absences on a paper roll. Over are the days of the business manager tracking leave on a ledger. To be able to manage the complexities of contemporary school life, systems and platforms must be able to 'talk' to each other by intersecting and sharing data.

The acting principal prior to my arrival had already selected two key platforms, an LMS and an SMS. One would house and share the curriculum, and the other would enable easy and detailed access to parent and student details. Both selections were excellent. My job was to make sure they were implemented well.

There nonetheless remained a number of operational areas that had no suitable system in place, or at best one that was ill-equipped to support us as we grew and became more sophisticated. This situation was purely due to the evolution of the school in its early-stage maturity.

I set about implementing new systems and platforms such as:

- Timetable software uploaded to our SMS to track the movement of every student and teacher
- An enrolment platform, also known as a funnel, that tracked enrolments from initial enquiry through to 'Welcome to Day 1 at Wisdom College'
- A College app to enable parents to receive quick and regular updates
- A vibrant, up-to-date and informative website that provided information for prospective parents and included a portal allowing current parents to access academic results
- A process for staff to submit absences of leave, purchase resources and request professional learning
- A transition from Google Docs and Gmail to Microsoft 365 and Outlook
- A process of teacher appraisal
- A marketing plan
- A risk register
- A budgeting system

We also needed to establish teams responsible for the core business of the school. We already had the Senior Leadership Team (SLT). To this we added the Student Wellbeing Committee (SWC) and the Teaching and Learning Committee (TLC). Smaller teams that met less regularly oversaw areas such as facilities, pastoral care and enrichment.

Drive curricular and co-curricular improvements and programs

Our primary school was well-established and had thorough curriculum plans, but our secondary school needed to catch up. We also lacked an overall curriculum map and subject-area maps. We set about building these documents, focusing on the secondary school in particular. I appointed a head of teaching and learning to drive these projects across P-12 and lead our academic programs in a developmental and sequential way.

The life of any school is enhanced by a strong co-curricular agenda that includes sport, music and a variety of activities such as debating and chess. As a Hizmet school, Wisdom also needed to establish a service-learning plan and an outdoor education program. Our camps program required consolidation and strengthening, and inter-school sporting competitions needed to be found for our kids to enter. To drive these initiatives, I appointed a head of co-curricular.

Implement frameworks

We needed two frameworks: one to help us teach curriculum content and one to help us care for our students and their families.

To articulate how we aimed to teach, bring content to life, impart knowledge and support all learners, we devised a curriculum philosophy. Grounded in the principles of differentiation and personalised learning, 'The Wisdom Way' was created under the leadership of our head of teaching and learning.

We were a Hizmet school, and we needed to live the humanitarian Hizmet principles. Our head of co-curricular created Wellbeing@Wisdom and the WISE Program to teach values and life skills.

Upgrade facilities

The state of our facilities was quite poor. Some of our demountable classrooms were dilapidated. Our verandas, pathways and disability ramps were non-compliant. There was insufficient seating, shade and storage. What we did have, though, was a hardworking and creative group of facility and ground staff who were itching to get stuck in.

Within three years we had installed:

- 11 new classrooms
- A multi-purpose court
- 2 courtyards with shade sails
- Approximately 100m of bench seating spread across the campus
- Lighting across the entire campus
- CCTV
- Fibre optic cables
- Pathways
- New primary school toilets
- Disability ramps
- 200 lockers
- A new phone system in all classrooms

And that was only the beginning. In a continued program of improvement, we:

- Relocated and refurbished a playground
- Demolished and removed a work shed and 4 old classrooms
- Created a master plan and planned for the construction of an 8-classroom double-storey building
- Built an outdoor classroom
- Levelled out the staff carpark
- Put down new veranda decking
- Painted the original old house on the schoolgrounds
- Planted approximately 100 new shrubs and trees

- Refurbished the undercroft area for parents to sit and chat in
- Renovated 3 existing classrooms
- Refurbished our science lab
- Rebuilt our art room
- Fixed up most of our plumbing
- Phased out Chromebooks and put everyone onto Microsoft-supported laptops
- Implemented a tuckshop system
- Dealt with too much paint, carpet, shelving, storage and landscaping to mention!

Set student expectations

Wisdom had fallen into the trap of accepting every student who applied—irrespective of their behavioural history, learning difficulties or socio-emotional dysfunctions. This was due partly to the fiscally responsive reason of needing to get bums on seats to attract government funding, partly to the lack of a clear enrolment funnel with benchmarks around what could be supported or tolerated, and partly to the College's unclear ambitions. Being inclusive and multicultural had become code for accepting everyone. In some cases, the school was a last resort for parents who could only afford low fees, didn't want to go to the public system and had a child who had been expelled from somewhere else. There was also a reluctance to remove students with ongoing histories of poor behaviour, socio-emotional issues and learning difficulties.

Further to this, the secondary school was only a few years into its establishment. Staff were making policy and decisions on the run without a roadmap or the experience needed to give it clear vision, leadership and management. So you can only imagine the scenes that I saw in classrooms, particularly secondary classrooms, on a daily basis. At times there was a sense of anarchy in the secondary school. Teachers felt powerless, lacking the confidence and skills to really take a stand. The students owned the space and we needed to take it back.

It was time for the senior leaders to act. We worked together to build a united front and a common plan.

I expelled two students in my first week, and another four by the end of my first term. These were students whose behaviour was unacceptable by anyone's standards.

We visited classrooms every day. I spent considerable time just sitting, observing and helping. I also unleashed fury upon any class that was being unruly, rude or disobedient. I did this to take back control, and to show teachers that they could do the same. We used the same methods to manage assemblies. Standards needed to be re-established.

We focused hard on uniform and on coming to class prepared. We gathered in the playground at the end of every break to herd the kids to class on time.

Roll out initiatives

Only once we had consolidated the fundamentals did we start to really explore new ways of doing education at Wisdom. We knew that the existing model was not catering to many of our students. Many of these kids were affected by fractured schooling histories, many had poor English literacy skills, some had parents who placed little importance on education and some had home environments that were unconducive to effective study.

So we implemented the following:

- Project Day—every Wednesday, students in Years 7 to 10 did one of four projects: Shark Tank, Workout Warriors, Interactive Museum and The Block. These projects were authentic and practical, including digital, verbal and written components. The Australian Curriculum was embedded within each. Each project had several pods and a pod master who facilitated their respective project.
- Early Friday finish for all students at 12.40pm—this allowed staff to meet, plan, collaborate and learn. I was determined to attract and retain staff, and to do this I needed to carve time out of the working week so as not to burden them with the need to complete these duties out of hours.
- Work from home for Year 11 and 12 students every Wednesday—senior students had the option to study at home, go to work or attend vocational training.

- Intensive literacy and numeracy workshops for students in Years 7 to 9. These classes were streamed based on ability.
- Year 10 Certificate 2 course in workplace skills—this gave our students a qualification, transferable skills and credit towards their senior certificate.

Mistakes made

I made plenty of mistakes, but these would be my big four:

- I lost sight of smaller details in my haste to implement, to improve, to change and to update. Some changes have come back to haunt me. I took the word of people who were acting with noble intentions but in hindsight didn't have the experience to provide the advice I needed. It's important to have the big-picture vision, but you can't take your eyes off the details—they matter.
- In redesigning the organisational chart, I dissolved some middle-management positions. I didn't fully acknowledge the time and effort that the people in these roles had put into them. I should have sat down, listened and talked things through with these people. I should have honoured the past much more.
- There were some staff whom I should have moved off the bus earlier, and there were some roles that I recruited for too quickly. I did this out of a scarcity mindset, as I knew how tight the market was for quality staff in the education sector. I should have been more patient.
- Within this multicultural setting with a large Muslim population, I should have spent more time learning the nuances of culture, faith and history. This remains a work in progress for me—in fact for all staff, I'd imagine.

Key takeaway

The iconic Robert Frost poem 'The Road Not Taken' provides me with the perfect analogy upon which to close this chapter. The poem ends with this sentence:

> *Two roads diverged in a wood, and I—*
> *I took the one less travelled by,*
> *And that has made all the difference.*

Established and well-resourced schools—those with strong reputations, wonderful facilities and kids who by virtue of their birth have all the advantages in life—tend to have no problem attracting excellent teachers and leaders. But who really needs the support of the educators drawn to these schools? The kids who come from disadvantage, from communities that are challenging and not as well-off. It's ironic that that those in greatest need of the best people, resources, support, programs and facilities don't get them. So if you are reading this and one day have the opportunity to do so—may I recommend that you take the road less travelled, for I guarantee that it will make all the difference to your life. There's a reason why this road is less travelled, and it's a gift to be able to find out why.

15

The future of school leadership

Lesson #16 *The future of schooling will see institutional shackles broken to create greater flexibility, choice and partnerships. Just as the classroom silo has opened up, so too in time will the school silo.*

If there was one good thing to emerge from Covid, it was that it forced the education sector to do things differently. The experience with virtual schooling showed teachers, parents and students that teaching and learning didn't need to be a face-to-face, sage-on-stage, content-in-content-out experience. Conversely, it also highlighted the impact of quality teachers, the value of human social interaction, the difficulty of providing remote learning support, the powerful role that the institution of schooling plays in the life of a family, and the importance of hands-on learning experiences.

It's true that plenty of places across the world were already experimenting with school design, alternate pathways and technology-augmented learning. I'd argue, though, that these practices were still viewed as outliers swimming upstream against the tide of convention. Covid lockdowns accelerated and expanded curiosities about different ways of doing things. People around the world began to demand models of schooling that met their needs and improved their quality of life. We will continue to see the education sector change in flexibility, choice, venues, programs, partnerships, teacher development and the design and structure of the school model.

A potted history of schooling

Before we peer into the future to predict the shape of mass education, let's look at its history. During the Middle Ages (c. 500AD–1500AD), various models of schooling could be found across the world in towns, churches, mosques and monasteries. Many of these schools were designed to provide instruction in skills useful for business or trade, but they also educated the next generation of religious clergy and followers. Needless to say, school wasn't compulsory and it certainly wasn't attended by all children.

Most of these children weren't learning in a class of up to 30 peers of roughly the same age. Knowledge was passed on to an individual or a small group. Those born into poverty, or at best the working class, did not come anywhere near what we would call an education by today's standards. In the late 1430s appeared perhaps the single most important invention to drag the human race out of the dark ages: the printing press. Think of it as the medieval internet!

Mass public education as we know it today started in the early 19th century. It was designed to provide two things: workers for the industrialised factory-based economy and childcare for the parents who were already working. Sure, the concept of providing an education to (or rather filling the heads of) young people in preparation for adulthood had been around for millennia. But this was only for a lucky few children born into families that could afford such luxuries, children whose parents or wider family deemed it important to educate them to one day assume a significant role in society, to continue the family business, to maintain the status quo. Rarely did girls receive an education comparable to that given to boys.

In modern times, it is fair to say that we've only seen real change in educational practices since the proliferation of the internet and personal devices. Both of these inventions have changed the way that students source information, consume content and reproduce knowledge. But how much have things really changed? Walk into most classrooms today and you'll still see kids at their desks with a teacher delivering content. The only difference is that there are laptops and a smart board instead of books and a chalk board. The tools have evolved, but the pedagogy hasn't.

With access to unlimited information and the ability to draw on all sorts of content sources, we thought that learning would reach the promised land. This, we imagined, was a place where all kids would be continuously engaged, where teachers would design brilliant lessons, where everything would be digitised and therefore easier to share and collaborate on. Instead, our literacy and numeracy levels have never been lower, the mental health of teenagers has never been worse, and teachers are leaving the profession in droves. We have significant challenges ahead of us, yet we keep doing what we've always done while expecting different results. As the quote goes, that's the definition of madness.

Forward-looking leadership

So what will characterise the future of learning, and what type of leadership will be required to support it?

Flexibility

Schools reflect society. The model of society has changed and the model of schooling should do the same. With both parents having to work in order to afford a mortgage, we aren't going to see a four-day week for primary schools anytime soon. If fact, schools could be doing more to support those parents who work beyond the hours of 9am–3pm.

There needs to be greater flexibility in:

- The school day and week
- The physical location of the teacher
- The pathways that students can follow—especially the senior years of schooling
- Student groupings—these should be based on competence and not solely on age

Choice

Online learning and ubiquitous access to content are available to everyone with an internet connection and a device. Some people see this as a solution to inequity in education, a way to reduce barriers and provide flexibility and choice for all regardless of personal wealth. In fact, it's only one part of the solution. Equally important are the habits for learning that are developed at an early age, and the value placed on education by parents. Children are strongly influenced by the home in which they are raised, and especially by the role-modelling and support provided by family. A student's socio-economic environment plays a big role in assisting them to attain a qualification and a well-paid career. Not every child will come from a family able to offer these opportunities. Collectively, school communities need to find ways for all children to have flexibility and affordable options. This means that we need to provide choice in how education is accessed and communicated, irrespective of location and context. It also means that we need to provide a choice of pathways for learning.

Pathways

Educational pathways should be hybrid and blended. Hybrid pathways open up a variety of options to students by allowing them to choose vocational courses as well as subjects that prepare them for university. Blended pathways allow students to work throughout the week, gaining experience and maybe even a small income while studying their choice of vocational or academic subjects. Through these pathways we develop work-ready young adults with a qualification and credit towards a university course should they wish to pursue it.

Some pathways may not be accessible to young people depending on the school they attend. But does this have to remain the case? Think about how we consume television today: we satisfy our interests by shifting between free-to-air channels and a variety of subscription services. The same concept can be applied to how we consume compulsory education.

In Australia, we're lucky to have a public education system that is generally well-resourced and delivers excellent outcomes. I'm sure some reading this may disagree, but as a teacher at a public school in a semi-rural location I found that we were very well catered for. Nevertheless, it cannot be denied that private, independent, fee-paying schools often have facilities, opportunities, staff and programs that give their students certain advantages in their lives and careers. Wouldn't it be great to not only have hybrid pathways, but also the ability to access courses from different schools through online learning? If one school delivers a physics course and another delivers biology, a student can do both.

Content and subjects

Learning areas have been curated over many centuries. We still teach quite defined and rigid subject matter that in many respects hasn't expanded a great deal. In recent years we've seen the emergence of subjects such as entrepreneurship, but if we took things a step further and considered topics such as youth mental health, global perspectives, sustainability, innovation, financial skills, disabilities and inclusion, aged care, loneliness and homelessness—now wouldn't that be interesting!

School day

Do students in Year 11 and 12 need five full days of school? Some schools (including Wisdom College) are changing this model to allow these students to study, work and pursue other interests and commitments. And do teachers need five full student-facing school days? Again, schools are finding innovative ways to carve time out of a typical school week for teachers to plan, collaborate, reflect, complete professional learning and do deep work. Within a typical timetable, do we need to spread one maths lesson per day across every week of the term? Is the adolescent brain really suited to changing gears four to six times a day? Why not have an intensive week of maths, assess and report, then move on to history? Do we need to keep students in classes based on their chronological age? Why not group them according to aptitude and ability, and assign specialist teachers to work with that group for a period of time? Yes, I know—this is called streaming, and schools have avoided it for valid reasons. But let's revisit it from another angle. Why not implement project-based learning based on interest? Projects that integrate subject matter instead of leaving it to be explored in silos? Projects that also integrate the life skills of teamwork and problem-solving while weaving in the general capabilities of literacy, numeracy and information technology? Plenty of schools have embraced this, but it's still not the norm. Let's do it more, and let's do it better.

Teachers

Teaching is still done largely in isolation. Teachers will plan collaboratively, but the task of teaching is generally a one-person approach. We need to think about teacher mentors, or at least teacher teams. Some primary classes might be lucky enough to have teacher aides, but it's just not the same. There needs to be a peer-to-peer relationship to share, collaborate and support. Teacher quality and job satisfaction are enhanced when teachers can be mentored by a respected person who has experience and the ability to provide feedback in a constructive manner. Providing this costs time and money, but the outcomes are immense.

Workforce

At the time of writing, educator profiles are quickly changing in the midst of an ongoing teacher recruitment problem. Put simply, there aren't enough teachers to fill the number of roles going around. There are, in fact, plenty of qualified teachers among the broader population. Most of these people choose not to teach despite completing a qualification, leave the profession to earn an income elsewhere, or have retired from the workplace completely. Averaging 20 or more years of teaching experience, school leaders are what you'd affectionately term the senior members of the profession. Rightly so, as it takes a bit of hard-earned knowledge to manage the complexities of school life. The problem is that this current group of educators did their training in the 1980s and 1990s. They are reaching retirement age or downsizing their careers towards less intense roles as they enter the final quarter of their working lives. With fewer teachers plying their trade and more school leaders leaving the hot seat, we have ourselves the perfect storm at the pointy end of the school management and leadership funnel.

This leads to a few things:

- A lack of senior educators with the experience to mentor younger colleagues on the skills of the teaching trade or school leadership

- Burnout for those leaders who are trying to hold it all together across a raft of staffing, social, behavioural and administrative challenges
- A lack of experienced educators who can lead large numbers of children, staff and parents with the wisdom and guile to make suitable decisions around welfare, facilities, staff, finances, learning and curriculum

We need to examine how we attract people to leadership, how we prepare them for it and how we retain them.

Principal as CEO

Some schools are now headed by CEO-style leaders instead of career educators. These people have plenty of experience in running a business, an enterprise or organisation, but none in teaching. This can work, but only with the assistance of deputies who have classroom knowledge. Teachers won't take advice from someone who doesn't have the lived experience of teaching 30 kids day after day while managing administrative and parental demands. If the CEO acknowledges this and can surround themselves with people who do have that sort of experience, then it can work quite well.

Hierarchies

There's no moving away from the hierarchical model of school leadership that has the principal at the top with a deputy reporting to them. What we are seeing already, though, is the separation of responsibilities. It is no longer possible for a principal to oversee everything. Depending upon the size of the school, you'll see a business manager and then a collection of deputies with the core responsibilities of curriculum, co-curricular, operations and administration.

The role of a principal is to coach, mentor, lead and manage those staff who directly report to them. If these people do their jobs well, everything else hums. No need to micro-manage them. They are there because someone hired them for their experience and skill. They are likely to be highly capable, autonomous, collaborative and driven individuals. Ideally, all a principal should need to do is to give them guidance, direction and resources and let them loose.

Demands of school leadership

School leaders need help. A large number of current teachers and middle leaders see principalship as unattractive, and it's easy to see why. The demands on heads of campus and deputies are also excessive. On a daily basis, school leaders are expected to manage very complex scenarios, social and family dysfunction, spiralling mental health challenges and a reduction in the number of staff available to teach and care for children. Not only is the curriculum to be dished out, but the emotional wellbeing of students is to be addressed. All of this takes place within a context of legal, compliance, HR, risk, administrative and WHS demands.

School leaders are constantly trying to balance multiple pressures. On the one hand, we have to deliver all the usual subjects, assessment and reporting related to national and state-mandated curricula. On the other, we also have to squeeze in lessons about life skills: responsible consumption of alcohol, safe driving, consent education, career education, cyber safety, resilience and grit. Then across all of these are key competencies, or work-ready skills, or skills for the 21st century—somewhat nebulous concepts such as problem-solving, collaboration, critical thinking, communication and decision-making. These competing priorities are usually led by staff who don't have a complete grasp of everything that's going on. Then, of course, we are being told that our national literacy and numeracy levels are declining, and are looking for the latest shiny magical fix to that problem.

We can't be all things to all people, and school can't be used as a catch-all device by governments and social activists. We've been doing this for some time, and the results are clear to see. We must make some tough decisions on what is to be covered by schools, and we need to change the current model of education to better serve the current model of student, family, work and society.

Training for school leadership

Mentoring and coaching are absolutely essential for middle and senior leaders, as well as those aspiring to leadership. This training needs to be intentional, structured and targeted. Like teachers, leaders should have professional development that addresses their weaknesses and includes goals that are both self-determined and expected by the school. Not all training can or should be done externally, as this is often expensive and takes people out of the school for an extended period of time. An investment in mentoring and coaching should be made by the principal, the board or the senior leadership team of the school, for the health of their own community as well as the profession.

> **Key takeaway**
>
> The future of schooling will be driven by choice and flexibility for students, parents and teachers alike. But innovation cannot exist without a solid foundational structure. If we want education to become more meaningful, more accessible and more efficient, we have a lot to address. If we want greater collaboration, we have to build trust. If we want to retain teachers, we have to make the profession attractive. If we want kids to stay engaged, we have to increase their options. Above all, we need courageous school leaders who are willing to try something new that challenges the status quo.

Conclusion

Lesson #17 *Good leadership is an accumulation of interactions and decisions that build people, strengthen relationships, and provide stability and direction.*

I admire anyone who willingly enters the fray of school leadership. Anyone who seeks the arena for the right reasons, as Teddy Roosevelt said all those years ago, has my respect. Whatever your role, the task of leadership is filled with challenges that will test anyone psychologically and physically. Facing these challenges has never been more important. Our school leaders are doing their best to manage a raft of workforce issues. We are seeing increasing rates of student disruption, violence and disengagement. Excessive administration and compliance have never been more pervasive. Nor can schools escape the influence of external political, social and economic tensions.

I've learnt just as much about school leadership from bad leaders as I have from good ones. A bad school leader puts their own desires first. They let their ego override their ability to care for others. They are not considerate or visible. They set the vision and see the big picture, but they neglect the little things and erode morale. They shy away from uncomfortable conversations or palm them off onto someone else. They don't make decisions, and when they do it's either without consultation or it's for the wrong reasons. They don't back their staff in the face of difficult students, parents or colleagues. They use bullying tactics to achieve results. They care more about their image than they do their people. They aren't approachable and they don't really listen. They have clear favourites, create silos among their colleagues and allow some staff to pursue pet projects that have no relevance to the greater good of the school.

Good leaders, on the other hand, do all or most of the things that I've revealed in this book. Sure, they don't always get it right, but the key difference is that they own their mistakes and keep working hard for the collective.

I wrote this book because I love my job and I love my profession. I want to do my part in assisting the next generation of school leaders. Too often, people who have shown some aptitude in teaching find themselves in leadership roles without the training, coaching or mentorship to succeed. If training is received, it is often on-the-job or simply acquired by osmosis. On top of that, it's often focused on the broad picture of creating strategy, building a team, managing change, growing trust or creating a vision. All worthwhile topics, without a doubt, but there's so much more to leadership. It's the everyday little things that mount up: the interactions in staffrooms, the presence in playgrounds, the regularity of communication, the bravery it takes to make a difficult decision, the sheer weight of responsibility, the crushing number of balls that need to be kept in the air, the hours that you put into the place at the expense of your own health, the sleepless nights when you are worried about how you'll pay salaries when you also have to install seating or shade or data projectors. In among this, you'll experience the delight of seeing an early-career teacher light up in front of a class for the first time. You'll feel the satisfaction of walking around a school and seeing dozens of children learning, laughing and socialising. You'll hear the hum of school life and feel completely at home. You'll see the eyes of parents glisten just a little when their child receives a certificate at assembly. You'll understand the value of being able to help a young person achieve something they'd only dreamed of. Yes, there is a price to pay for school leadership, but the rewards are well worth it.

When we do throw someone into the arena, it's helpful to give them a few weapons to be competitive in the contest. Well-equipped school leaders help all tiers of the school community. It's my hope that this book has provided you with advice that is practical and can be applied quickly. However, if nothing else sticks, my top pieces of advice to wrap things up will follow this chapter. Think of them as the rules of the leadership game.

Print them off, write them down, put them in a place where you can see them regularly. When you are in the arena and the combatants are circling and the uncertainty is creeping in, they may just give you the clarity and courage you need.

The 15 rules of the leadership game

1. Your core desire should not only be to build people, but also to back people.
2. Much like how a teacher needs to build a relationship and rapport with their class before learning can happen, a leader needs to build trust with their people before change and growth can happen.
3. There's nothing wrong with personal goals, but collective goals are more powerful.
4. What you accept becomes your standard, so you need to set the standard.
5. Be comfortable in being disliked, because simply doing what you are hired to do will upset some people.
6. Admit mistakes, ask for help, be vulnerable and allow others to do the same.
7. Your words are meaningless if they are not reinforced by your actions.
8. Continue to learn, cultivate curiosity, mine for different opinions and encourage these qualities in your team.
9. Do what's right, not what's popular or follows the path of least resistance; opt for short-term pain and long-term gain every time.
10. Hire for attitude before aptitude. Content and skills can be taught, character and morals cannot.

11. When you accept the leadership badge, you choose to step into the arena—if you aren't prepared to step in and stay in, then do us all a favour and step aside.
12. There's nothing soft about soft skills—they are the hardest part of leadership.
13. Follow the KIT principle of kindness, inclusion and transparency. Most other things take care of themselves if you do these things consistently.
14. You've got to have a plan. Know what you can change and what you can't, then get stuck in.
15. Do the hard carry. In rugby league, this refers to the player who carries the ball into the opposition defence when they are on their own try line. They know that they will get smashed, but they do it anyway and with boundless energy, for the greater good of the team. What are you prepared to do to achieve success and positive outcomes for your students, staff and community? How bad do you really want it? Because if it's worth having, it's worth fighting for.

References

Browning, P. (2020). *Principled.* University of Queensland Press. Brisbane.

Collins, J. (2001). *Good to Great: Why Some Companies Make the Leap... and Others Don't.* HarperCollins. New York.

Frost, R., Lathem, E. C., & Lathem, E. C. (1979). *The poetry of Robert Frost: the collected poems, complete and unabridged.* H. Holt. New York.

Kerr, J. (2015). *Legacy: What the All Blacks Can Teach Us about the Business of Life.* Constable. London.

King, S. (1982). *Rita Hayworth and Shawshank Redemption.* Hodder. London.

Sinek, S. (2017). *Leaders Eat Last: Why Some Teams Pull Together and Others Don't.* Penguin. London.

Stanier, M. B. (2016). *The Coaching Habit: Say Less, Ask More, and Change the Way You Lead Forever.* Box of Crayons Press. Toronto.

Thomas, D. (2026). *The Collected Poems of Dylan Thomas: The Centenary Edition.* (Ed. John Goodby). Weidenfeld & Nicolson. London.

Tracy, B. (2004). *Eat That Frog: Get More of the Important Things Done.* Hodder. London.

Whitmore, J. (2009). *Coaching for performance: GROWing human potential and purpose: The principles and practice of coaching and leadership* (4th ed). Nicholas Brealey Publishers. London.

Acknowledgments

To the staff, students and community of Wisdom College.

It's only through partnership, relationships, patience and humour that we have as a team managed to provide an environment where we can learn, grow, feel safe, argue yet still be loved and create a space that gives all of us a fighting chance at this thing called life.

Thank you for including me, supporting me and having the courage to question the status quo.

Thank you especially to my Wisdom mates: Canan Coskun, Ayse Dogan, James Easthope, Mark Richards, Radha Devi, Olivia Starkey, Grace Li, Esma Turk, Aliya Wazir, Amanda Nicholls and Ali Halloum. I love you guys and will never forget.

About the author

Damien is a career educator. Some would say he is somewhat institutionalised, as he went from high school to university then back to high school and never left! He'd have it no other way.

Starting in the mid-1990s, his career has spanned almost 30 years. Now a principal, Damien has worked in a variety of schools: primary, secondary, public, independent, all-girls, all-boys and co-ed. He's always been a classroom teacher and remains one to this day. He's been a deputy headmaster and college principal, has coordinated year levels, led schools and departments and headed campuses spanning two states.

Damien has an MBA and a Doctorate in Education. His thesis investigated best practices in teacher appraisal mechanisms. Being awarded a Churchill Fellowship afforded him the opportunity to travel the world to research and create rite-of-passage programs for teenage boys to reduce incidences of domestic violence. Damien aims to one day finish his career where it all started: in the classroom.

www.ingramcontent.com/pod-product-compliance
Lightning Source LLC
LaVergne TN
LVHW020134080526
838202LV00047B/3933